The iPod touch
PocketGuide

Christopher**Breen**

Ginormous knowledge, pocket-sized.

Peachpit
Press

The iPod touch Pocket Guide
Christopher Breen

Peachpit Press
1249 Eighth Street
Berkeley, CA 94710
510/524-2178
510/524-2221 (fax)

Find us on the Web at: www.peachpit.com
To report errors, please send a note to errata@peachpit.com.

Peachpit Press is a division of Pearson Education.

Executive editor: Clifford Colby
Editor: Kathy Simpson
Production editor: David Van Ness
Compositor: Myrna Vladic
Indexer: Ann Rogers
Cover design: Peachpit Press
Cover image: Mike Tanamachi
Screen photo: iStockphoto
Interior design: Peachpit Press

ISBN-13:   978-0-321-68045-7
ISBN-10:   0-321-68045-6

9 8 7 6 5 4 3 2

Printed and bound in the United States of America

To my Doodle-Jumpin' girl, Addie.

About the Author

Christopher Breen has been writing about technology since the latter
days of the Reagan administration for such publications as *MacUser,
MacWEEK,* and *Macworld.* Currently a senior editor for *Macworld,* Breen
pens its popular "Mac 911" tips-and-troubleshooting column and blog,
routinely opines about digital media in its Playlist blog, and hosts the
Macworld Podcast. He's also the author of Peachpit's *The iPhone Pocket
Guide, The iPod & iTunes Pocket Guide,* and *The Flip Mino Pocket Guide.*
When not engaged in technological pursuits, he's a professional musi-
cian in the San Francisco Bay Area.

Acknowledgments

This book would not be in your hands (or, if you're that sort of person, on your e-book reader) if not for the dedication of the following people.

At Peachpit Press: Publisher Nancy Ruenzel, who continues to support these efforts; Cliff Colby, who graciously agreed to give the iPod touch a book of its own; Kathy Simpson, who, as usual, did everything that needed doing after the manuscript left my computer and took up residence on hers (we make a hell of a team!); production pro David Van Ness, who, with barely an anxious ripple, turned our work into the lovely book you hold now; Myrna Vladic, who made words and pictures fit so attractively within the confines of these pages; and Rebecca Plunkett, who performed a book's most thankless yet necessary job: indexing.

At home: My wife, Claire, who put up with the missed nights and weekends that come with putting together not just one book, but two; and my daughter, Addie, who gave her father a huge smile and welcome hug at the end of every working day.

Abroad: *Macworld* Editorial Director Jason Snell, who never said, "I'd like exclusive rights to that brain full of iPod goodness"; the folks at Lynda.com for their patience; and the boys from System 9 for their continued cool-cattedness.

And, of course, the sleep-deprived designers, engineers, and other Apple folk who gave birth to the original iPod touch and the software that runs it, and the countless developers who make the iPod touch a more wonderful hunk of technology with each passing day.

Contents

Getting Started

So you have a new iPod touch. Congratulations! It's a wonderful piece of technology, and you're going to love it.

Understanding just how eager you are to dig in and play with this new object of your affection, I've put together a few pages devoted to getting your iPod touch up and running in the shortest time possible. Just follow these steps:

1. Look at the box.

   If the box tells you that you have an iPod classic, iPod nano, or iPod shuffle, return this book for a copy of my *The iPod & iTunes Pocket Guide* (Peachpit Press); this book focuses only on the iPod touch. If the box has *iPhone* plastered across the front, you'll want to delve instead into my *The iPhone Pocket Guide* (also from Peachpit Press); again, this book is about the iPod touch. If the box reads *Macaroni and Cheese*, open it; boil the pasta for 9 minutes (add 2 minutes for higher altitudes); toss in a tablespoon of milk, pat of butter, and powdered cheese sauce; stir; and enjoy. Then pick up the other box that has the words *iPod touch* printed on it.

2. Open the box.

   No, the iPod touch hasn't been switched on since it left the factory. There's a plastic sticker over the top of the display that shows the touch's interface. Peel off that sticker; then you can remove the iPod from its mounting tray.

3. Install iTunes.

   If you don't already have a current copy of iTunes on your computer, download it from www.apple.com/itunes/download. (Apple hasn't bundled a CD copy of iTunes with the iPod for quite some time.) Follow whatever onscreen directions are necessary to put iTunes on your Windows PC or Mac.

4. Connect the iPod to your computer.

   You're welcome to click the iPod's Home button (the single round button at the bottom of the display), but if the iPod is charged, all you'll see is a picture of a connector cable pointing to an icon of the iTunes application. This picture is a very broad hint that your new iPod touch isn't going to do much more than tempt you with its untapped talents until you plug it into your computer. Not much satisfaction in that, is there?

   Remove the Dock-connector cable from the box; then attach the wider end to the bottom of the iPod and the squatter end to a powered USB 2.0 port on your Mac or Windows PC. This cable is the means for both charging the iPod and transferring data between it and your computer.

5. Register your iPod (or don't).

   After you install iTunes and attach the iPod to your computer, iTunes should launch automatically. If it doesn't, launch it.

   When iTunes sees a brand-new iPod or one that's been restored (reformatted), it helps you register and set up the device. The first screen you see will offer you a choice: register now by clicking a Continue button, or register later by clicking a button that says, of all things, Register Later. When you register, you'll be asked to acknowledge a license agreement.

6. Obtain an Apple ID.

   Whether or not you choose to register your iPod, you'll be prompted to enter an existing Apple ID or create a new one. Having an Apple ID allows you to download and purchase media from the iTunes Store and applications from the App Store directly to your iPod touch.

   note **You need a credit card number to procure an Apple ID.**

   After dealing with the Apple ID screen, you may also be asked whether you'd like to sign up for Apple's $100-a-year MobileMe service—an online suite that includes an email account; online storage; online picture and video galleries; a Web-based calendar and address book; and synchronization of your email messages, contacts, and calendars across all your computers and mobile devices (including the iPod touch). This service is purely optional.

7. Choose a setup option.

   A Set Up Your iPod screen will appear, offering one or two options. The first option is Set Up As New iPod. If you've never attached an iPod touch or iPhone to this computer, choose this option and click Continue.

   When you do, if you already have some music in your iTunes Library, you'll be offered options to do several things automatically: sync songs and videos to the iPod, add photos to it, and sync any applications you currently have in your iTunes Library (as you might if you've already downloaded some applications from the App Store in anticipation of acquiring your new iPod). iTunes will honor your choices if it can fit everything into your iTunes Library on the iPod. If you have more music in your library than will fit on the iPod, iTunes will sync a portion of the music to the iPod—just music; no videos or pictures.

If you've previously synced an iPod touch or iPhone with this computer, you'll see the additional option to restore the currently attached iPod touch from a backup from one of these previously attached devices. (Yes, you can restore data from an iPhone to an iPod touch.) If multiple backups are available, they appear in the pop-up menu next to this option; just choose the one you want.

As all this is happening, the words *Sync in Progress* appear on your iPod's display.

8. Rip a CD.

You say you have no music in your iTunes Library? No worries. I'll show you how to put some in it.

When I suggest that you rip a CD, I don't mean physically rip the disc in half. *Rip* in this context means to copy the audio from the CD to your computer. To do this, insert the disc into your computer's CD or DVD drive, and launch iTunes (if it doesn't launch automatically after you insert the disc). By default, iTunes 7 and later tosses up a dialog box that asks "Would you like to import the CD *NameofCD* into your iTunes library?" (where *NameofCD* is the name of your disc). Click Yes, and iTunes converts the audio files to a format that can be played on the iPod. Also, the tracks you ripped from the CD appear in iTunes' main window when you click the Music entry in the iTunes Source list.

To import the CD at a later time, click No in this dialog box. Then, later, with that disc in the drive, select it in the Source list (it appears below the Devices heading), and click the Import CD button in the bottom-right corner of the iTunes window.

9. Copy some music to your iPod.

If the only music you have in your iTunes Library is that which you just ripped from the CD, you need to move it to your iPod. To do this, select your iPod in iTunes' Source list, click the Music tab in the main window, click the Sync Music option, and choose Entire Music Library. Click the Apply button in the bottom-right corner of the iTunes window; then click the Sync button that now appears there. The music is copied to your iPod.

10. Unmount and play.

When the music has finished transferring, locate the name of your iPod in iTunes' Source list (it, too, appears below the Devices heading), and click the little Eject icon next to it. When the iPod disappears from iTunes, unplug it from your computer.

tip **This is the "good practice" method for ejecting the iPod, because it allows iTunes to finish whatever business it has with the iPod before unmounting it. Unlike other iPods, however, the touch lets you unceremoniously unplug it from your computer without getting an iTunes complaint in the form of a terse dialog box.**

Unwrap the earbuds that came with the iPod, jam them into your ears, and plug the other end into the iPod's headphone port on the bottom of the iPod. If you have a new 32 GB or 64 GB iPod touch, take a look at the cord dangling from the right earbud. That rectangular gray object you see is the headphone controller for your iPod. Press the middle of this controller, and your iPod will play music.

If you have a new 8 GB iPod touch, an older iPod touch that doesn't include headphones with a controller, or a different set of headphones that likewise lacks a controller, click the iPod's Home button, and slide your finger to the right where you see the words *Slide to Unlock*. This action grants you access to your iPod's touchscreen controls.

Tap the Music icon in the bottom-left corner of the iPod's screen. You'll be taken to a Playlists screen. Tap the Songs icon at the bottom of this screen and then tap the name of a song on the resulting Song screen. The song you tapped will start playing. The Now Playing screen that appears may even display artwork for the song.

To increase the volume, press the top of the headphone controller (if you have one); press the top of the volume toggle switch on the left side of the iPod; or, if you're looking at the Now Playing screen on the iPod, tap the silver ball in the volume slider at the bottom of the display and drag your finger to the right. To decrease the volume, press the bottom of the headphone controller (again, if present); press the bottom of the toggle switch on the side of the iPod; or tap and drag to the left on the volume slider in the Now Playing screen.

11. Enjoy.

Relax and let the music wash over you. When you're ready to explore the iPod touch's many other wonders, read on.

Charge It (If Necessary)

If the iPod doesn't work out of the box, you need to charge it up. You can do this by plugging the included USB cable into your computer's powered USB 2.0 port and plugging the other end of the cable into the bottom of the iPod. If you have a charger for your iPod (chargers are optional for all iPods), you can plug the cable's USB connector into the charger instead of your computer, plug the other end of the cable into your iPod, and plug the charger into a wall socket. (Chargers for older iPods that use a FireWire connector won't charge the iPod touch.)

Meet the iPod touch

In the early summer of 2007, Apple released a little something called the iPhone. Maybe you've heard of it. With the iPhone came the promise of an iPod that could be controlled not by a wheel or series of buttons, but the touch of a finger. A few months later, the iPod touch delivered on that promise. A year after that, an updated second-generation (2G) version with a volume switch and an internal speaker appeared. Fast-forward one more year, and there appeared a new iPod touch, similar to the previous year's 2G iPod touch but with a faster processor and graphics chip.

The iPod touch is sort of a hybrid between a regular iPod and the iPhone. Like the iPhone, the iPod touch bears a touchscreen display that you control by tapping, flicking, pinching, and dragging objects on its screen. (See Chapter 2 for more information on controlling your touch.) It also includes wireless networking circuitry (Wi-Fi). It has the same media capabilities as the iPhone, letting you play music and videos, view slide-shows, and watch YouTube videos streamed across the Web. And just as you can with an iPhone, you can purchase music and third-party applications directly from the iPod touch via the device's version of Apple's iTunes Store and App Store, respectively.

The touch also includes all the iPhone's non-phone-related applications: Safari, Calendar, Mail, Contacts, YouTube, Stocks, Maps, Weather, Clock, Calculator, Voice Memos, and Notes. Because you can't make a call with the iPod touch, there's no need for the iPhone's SMS application (which is called Messages) or any of the phone features.

As this book goes to press, the iPod touch comes in capacities of 8 GB, 32 GB, and 64 GB, priced at $199, $299, and $399, respectively. The 8 GB model is actually the original 2G iPod touch. The 32 GB and 64 GB iPod touches are the new design that includes the faster processor and graphics chip.

Apple claims that the 8 GB touch will hold up to 1,750 4-minute songs encoded in AAC format at 128 Kbps. (I explain all this encoding stuff in Chapter 3.) The 32 GB model can hold up to 7,000 audio tracks encoded the same way. And you'll smush 14,000 songs onto a 64 GB touch. A 2-hour movie purchased from the iTunes Store consumes around 1.3 GB, and an hourlong TV show (really, around 43 minutes when the commercials have been stripped out) eats up close to 500 MB. Given the girth of these videos, it's clear that you're not going to pack the entire *Pink Panther* oeuvre plus four seasons of *Lost* onto your lower-capacity iPod touch.

Like all iPods, the touch is powered by a rechargeable lithium-ion polymer battery. Apple suggests that the iPod touch can play music continuously for up to 30 hours and video for up to 6 hours. Your actual mileage will vary, however, depending on whether you have Wi-Fi switched on or off. (Wi-Fi consumes a fair amount of battery power even when it's supposedly doing nothing.)

Great iPod, Pocket Computer, Portable Game Player

The descriptive words above—*Great iPod, Pocket Computer, Portable Game Player*—are exactly the terms Apple uses to describe the iPod touch. How does it live up to those descriptions?

- **Great iPod? Yes.** Indeed, I consider a slim, pocketable device that provides a unique touchscreen interface for browsing your music collection by album cover and a beautifully bright 3.5-inch display on which you can view pictures, TV shows, music videos, video podcasts, and movies in a widescreen way to be pretty darned great. Thanks to the inclusion of the iTunes Store on the iPod touch, you can even purchase music and video and download it directly to the iPod over a Wi-Fi connection.

- **Great pocket computer? Yes.** When the iPhone was first released, pundits (me among them) debated whether it was a phone or a computer that just happened to make calls. With the iPod touch, you needn't split hairs. It's clearly a small computer that also happens to be a perfectly wonderful media player. Right out of the box, the touch lets you surf the Web, send and receive email, plot a course with the Maps application, check stocks and weather, view YouTube videos, and compose notes.

  Should the built-in applications not be enough, there's always the App Store. Need a wireless remote control for your iTunes Library or Apple TV? Apple's free Remote application for the iPod touch and iPhone provides it. Want to learn about all the restaurants within a 10-mile radius? You can get apps for that too. Care to send an instant message to a friend? Just turn to one of the instant-messaging clients available from the App Store. Need to send a quick tweet or update your Facebook page? Yes, there are apps for that. The possibilities are nearly endless, as the App Store's more than 75,000 apps (as I write this chapter) attest.

- **Great portable game player? Increasingly so.** Apple is pushing hard in many directions to make the iPod touch *the* portable gaming system to own. It's doing this not only by spreading the word to its customers, but also by reaching out to developers such as Electronic Arts, Ubisoft, id Software, and Gameloft to make great games available for the iPod touch and iPhone. In the first months of the App Store's existence, a lot of iPod touch and iPhone games were released, and a lot of them weren't very good. Given the number of apps at the App Store, there will always be a large number of mediocre games. What's new is that now there's a solid selection of truly outstanding games.

- **And more? Yes.** Add to all those features the iPod touch's unique multi-touch screen, which lets you use natural finger motions and virtual onscreen controls to manage your iPod; a sensor that detects the iPod's vertical or horizontal orientation and rotates its images accordingly; and built-in Wi-Fi and Bluetooth capability, and you've got a fairly formidable hunk of technology in your pocket.

Oh, and did I mention that the iPod touch works with both Windows PCs and Macs? Or that the computer application that handles the handshake between your computer and the iPod touch is one you're already familiar with? Yes, that would be the same iTunes you now use to load your old iPod with music, podcasts, games, movies, and TV shows.

In this inaugural chapter, I look at the items that come in the iPod touch box, as well as the physical features and controls that make up this three-in-one wonder.

Boxed In

The clear box holds more than the iPod touch. Within, you'll find these goodies.

iPod touch

Well, of course. You didn't lay out $200, $300, or $400 with the dream of getting an electric shaver, did you? There, clipped to its plastic tray, is your iPod.

Earphones

Your iPod comes with a set of earphones that you place inside—rather than over—your ears. Earphones of this style are known as *earbuds*. Which set of earphones you receive depends on the iPod touch model you purchase.

If you purchased an 8 GB model (the previous year's 2G iPod touch), you get Apple's standard earbuds—the kind you'd get with an iPod classic. If you purchased a 32 GB or 64 GB iPod touch, you'll find in the box the same earphones that ship with today's iPhone. What distinguishes the latter earphones is the small gray plastic controller embedded in the right earbud's cord (**Figure 1.1**). This controller includes a microphone for recording voice memos and issuing voice commands, as well as three buttons: Volume Up, Volume Down, and a Center button for controlling audio and video playback.

Figure 1.1
The iPod touch's headset controller.

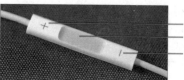

Volume Up
Center
Volume Down

Here are some uses for this controller:

- To adjust the volume of the headset, press the Volume Up button to increase volume or the Volume Down button to turn things down. These volume buttons aren't of the press-and-hold variety; volume goes up or down only when you press and release the button. To increase volume by two increments, press the top button twice in succession.

- While listening to music or watching a video, press the Center button once to pause playback.

- Press it twice to move to the next track when listening to music.

- Press it three times in succession to move to the previous track when listening to music.

- Press the switch twice in rapid succession while you're watching a video, and if the video has chapter markers, you'll skip to the next chapter. (If the video has no chapters, nothing happens.) If you press three times in rapid succession while watching a video with chapters, you move back to the beginning of the currently playing chapter. Stop playback with a single click and press the switch three times quickly, and you go back to the previous chapter.

- Press and hold the Center button for a couple of seconds to call up the Voice Control screen. This feature lets you control the iPod touch's music functions with your voice. (I discuss all that is Voice Control in Chapter 3.)

Documentation

Beneath the plastic tray are three hunks of paper: a Getting Started guide; a safety information guide, which you may be able to read if you wear 6x reading glasses; and a sheet that bears two white Apple stickers, appropriate for placing anywhere you want to let your Apple flag fly.

Dock connector-to-USB cable

You string this cable between the Dock-connector port on the bottom of the iPod or a Dock (if you have one) and either the USB power adapter or a USB port on your computer. When it's connected to a computer, this cable acts as both data and power link between the iPod and computer. Without it, you can't sync media and information from the computer to the iPod, as the iPod—Wi-Fi wonder though it may be—syncs only via the cable.

On the Face of It

Thanks to its touchscreen display, the iPod sports very few buttons and switches. Those that it does possess, however, are important (**Figure 1.2**).

Figure 1.2

The iPod touch provides exactly the buttons, switches, and ports you need without cluttering its elegant design.

COURTESY OF APPLE, INC.

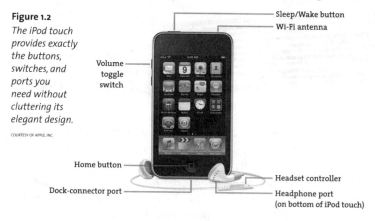

Sleep/Wake button
Wi-Fi antenna
Volume toggle switch
Home button
Dock-connector port
Headset controller
Headphone port
(on bottom of iPod touch)

Up front

After removing the iPod touch from its tray and flipping it in your hand a time or two, you'll come to a remarkable realization: The thing apparently has but one button! No Play, Rewind, Fast Forward, Blend, Mix, Grill—just an indented round button at the bottom of the display. This button is the Home button, and as its name implies, it takes you to the iPod's Home screen nearly every time you click it once.

(OK, I'll end the suspense: You also use the Home button to wake up your sleeping iPod. When you do, you don't go home; rather, after unlocking the iPod, you see the last screen that was visible when the iPod dozed off. Also, when you're already looking at the first screen of the Home screen and you click this button, you're taken to the Spotlight screen, where you can search for items on your iPod.)

Click it quickly twice in succession, however, and its behavior changes, depending on how you've set up the Home button—a topic that I examine more closely in Chapter 2.

On top

Look a little more carefully, and you discover a few more mechanical controls and ports. On the top edge of the iPod touch is a tiny black button. Apple describes this thing as the Sleep/Wake button, which you also use to turn the iPod on and off.

To lock the iPod, press this button. (To unlock the iPod, click the Home button and slide your finger where you see the words *Slide to Unlock*.) To switch the iPod off, press and hold the Sleep/Wake button for a few seconds until a red slider, labeled *Slide to Power Off*, appears onscreen. Drag the slider to the right to switch off the iPod (or tap Cancel to belay that order). "Drag?" you ask. Yes, the gesture is exactly what it sounds like. Place your finger on the arrow button and slide it to the right. (I describe all these maneuvers in the "Full Gestures" section later in this chapter.)

To turn the iPod on after shutting it off, press and hold the Sleep/Wake button until you see the Apple logo on the display.

Down below

Smack-dab in the middle of the iPod touch's bottom edge is the familiar-to-iPod-owners Dock-connector port. This port is a proprietary 30-pin connector used for syncing the iPod and attaching such accessories as power adapters, FM transmitters, and speaker systems.

To the right of the Dock-connector port is the headphone port, which accommodates the iPod's white headset plug.

To the left

The original iPod touch had no physical volume buttons. If you wanted to adjust its volume, you had to do so using the touchscreen. Enough people complained about the inability to adjust the touch's volume from within a pocket (a nice idea when you're rocking out in arctic breezes) that with the 2G iPod touch, Apple placed volume controls on the iPod. You find these controls along the left side of the iPod in the form of a Volume rocker switch. Press it up to increase the volume; press it down to decrease the volume.

The back

Other than the Apple logo, the iPod name, the iPod's capacity, and some really tiny print, the only thing you'll find on the back of the iPod is the black plastic that marks its Wi-Fi antenna. If you're a fan of funhouse mirrors, feel free to check your look in the iPod's polished chrome case.

note And by *the only thing*, I do mean that you won't find a lever, switch, or button to open the iPod for the purpose of replacing its battery. Like other iPods and the iPhone, the iPod touch doesn't offer a user-replaceable battery. When your iPod's battery gives up the ghost, you must have it serviced. See Chapter 9 for more on the iPod's battery.

Icon See That

When operating your iPod, you'll see a variety of small icons in its status bar. Here's what they mean:

Wi-Fi. This icon indicates that you're connected to a Wi-Fi network. The stronger the signal, the more bars you see.

VPN. The iPod displays this symbol if you're connected to a VPN (virtual private network).

Network activity. If your iPod is busy syncing or talking to a network, you see the Mac OS X–like "I'm doing something" symbol.

Lock. Your iPod is locked.

Play. Your iPod is playing music.

Alarm. You've set an alarm.

Bluetooth. If you see a blue or white Bluetooth icon, the iPod is linked to a Bluetooth device. If you see a gray Bluetooth icon, Bluetooth is on, but the iPod's not linked to a Bluetooth device.

Battery. This icon indicates the battery level and charging status. A battery icon with a lightning bolt tells you that the iPod is charging. When you see a battery icon with a plug icon, the battery is connected to a power supply and fully charged. A battery icon without a lightning-bolt or plug icon tells you that the iPod isn't plugged into power. The solid portion of the battery icon tells you approximately how much power is left in the battery.

Applications

As I write these words, Apple bundles 19 applications with today's iPod touch. You access these applications from the iPod's Home screen, which you can summon easily by clicking the Home button on the face of the iPod.

The Docked Four

At the bottom of the iPod touch is a Dock housing four applications that Apple thinks important enough to highlight by placing them in this prominent position.

Music

Well, this device *is* an iPod, after all, so the Music app deserves this kind of attention. This app is what you use to play music, audio podcasts, and audiobooks. I cover this application extensively in Chapter 3.

Videos

The iPod touch wouldn't be much of a media player if it didn't play videos. This application takes on that chore, playing movies, TV shows, music videos, video podcasts, and other compatible videos that you sync to the device. I describe this area in Chapter 3 as well.

Safari

Safari is Apple's Web browser. Just like the iPhone, the iPod touch carries a real live Web browser rather than a "baby browser" that grudgingly allows you to view only a small portion of the material a Web page offers. When you pull up a Web page in the iPod's Safari, it looks and behaves like a real Web page. Chapter 6 is devoted to Safari.

The App Store

As I mention earlier in this chapter, the applications you place on your iPod touch can make it a far more powerful and entertaining device. Although you can obtain these applications via iTunes, you can also download them directly over Wi-Fi from your iPod touch. The App Store is the means for doing that. I write about this store as well as the iTunes Store in Chapter 4.

The Other 13 (plus 2)

The built-in applications don't stop with the Docked Four. The iPod touch includes other applications that handle things like email, photos, calendars, stocks, and weather.

Mail

This application is the iPod touch's email client. As with the email client on your computer, you use the iPod's Mail app to compose and send messages, as well as to read and manage received email. I look at Mail in Chapter 5.

Calendar

When you sync your iPod touch, you can transfer calendar events and alarms from Apple's iCal and from Microsoft's Entourage and Outlook. If you have a MobileMe or Microsoft Exchange account, you can sync the calendar information from these services automatically over the air. These transferred and synced items appear in the iPod's Calendar application. You can also add events directly to the iPod by using the iPod's keyboard and then sync those events with your computer or a MobileMe or Exchange server. I discuss Calendar in more detail in Chapter 5.

Photos

Tap the Photos icon, and you see a collection of all the images you've captured with the iPod's built-in screen-capture feature, as well as those photos that you've synced to your iPod via iTunes. Chapter 7 offers more details on the iPod's photo capabilities.

Contacts

The iPod touch can hold all the contacts in your computer's address-book application. Additionally, you can create contacts of your own, as well as automatically sync contacts from MobileMe or an Exchange server. Look for more about Contacts in Chapter 5.

YouTube

With this application, you can view streamed YouTube videos on your iPod. YouTube, being a visual-based application, is examined in Chapter 7.

Stocks

Similar to the Stocks widget in Apple's Mac OS X, the iPod's Stocks application lets you track your favorite stocks in near real time. All widgety things are detailed in Chapter 8.

Maps

Lost? A street map is just a tap away. Based on Google Maps, this application quickly provides not only maps, but also current driving conditions, satellite views, and the locations of businesses within each map. Chapter 8 covers the Maps app.

Weather

Much like another Mac OS X widget, the Weather application displays current conditions, as well as the six-day forecasts for locations of your choosing. Like I said, Chapter 8 is great.

Voice Memos

Voice Memos allows you to record audio through the microphone planted in the iPod's headset or from a compatible third-party mic. You just know that I'm going to discuss it in Chapter 8.

Notes

Notes is the iPod touch's tiny text editor. Use the iPod's virtual keyboard to create lists, jot down reminders, compose haiku, or remind yourself to look in Chapter 8 for more details.

Clock

Find the time anywhere in the world, as well as create clocks of favorite locations. You also use the Clock application to create alarms and to invoke the stopwatch and countdown timer. Yeah, see Chapter 8 for this one too.

Calculator

Still can't figure out an appropriate tip without using your fingers? Pull up the iPod's Calculator to perform common math operations (and, with the Scientific Calculator view that appears when you turn the iPod to a horizontal position, not-so-common math operations too). You're not going to make me write it again, are you? *Sigh*. OK, Chapter 8.

iTunes

The final application in the Home screen, iTunes, is the iPod touch's version of the iTunes Store. With this small but powerful app and a Wi-Fi broadband connection, you can download music, movies, TV shows, music videos, audiobooks, and iTunes U content. I look at the iTunes app along with the other stores in Chapter 4.

Settings

Settings is one of the "Plus 2" applications in this list. Though Settings technically isn't an application, a tap of the Settings icon produces a preferences window for configuring such features as Wi-Fi, data fetching, sounds, brightness, wallpaper, general settings (including date and time, autolock, password lock, network, Bluetooth, and keyboard), mail, Safari, music, video, and photos. Some third-party applications plant their settings in this screen as well. Though I discuss Settings with regard to specific applications throughout this little tome, I provide the big picture in Chapter 2.

Nike + iPod

You've dutifully counted all the icons on your iPod touch's Home screen, and you've come up with 18. Ah, but have you gone to the Settings screen, tapped Nike + iPod, and toggled this feature on? If you have, you've been reading ahead. Shame on you! This app is the other "Plus 2" application. I talk about Nike + iPod in Chapter 2.

Full Gestures

The iPod's screen is deliberately touchy: Touching it is how you control the device. This section covers the gestures you use to navigate and control your iPod.

Tap

You're going to see the word *tap* a lot in this book. When you want to initiate an action—launch an application, control the iPod's media-playback features, flip a object around, or move to the next screen—this gesture is the one you'll likely use. If you've turned on the iPod's VoiceOver accessibility features—a feature that helps the visually and aurally impaired use the device—a single tap selects an item. I cover accessibility in Chapter 2.

Tap and hold

You use the tap-and-hold gesture when editing text—either to bring up the magnifying-glass icon to help insert a cursor or to initiate the process for cutting, copying, and pasting text. The iPod touch 3.0 software introduced cut, copy, and paste to the iPod, allowing you to work more readily with text or Web-site content. See "Text Entry and Editing" later in this chapter for more on cut, copy, and paste.

Double tap

Sometimes, just one tap won't do. Double-tapping often enlarges or contracts an image—zooms in on a photo or Web-page column, for example, or returns it to its normal size after you've enlarged it. Other times, it can make items return to the previous view.

When the VoiceOver feature is on, a double tap acts like a single tap ordinarily does. With VoiceOver engaged, one tap tells you what you're touching, and a double tap launches the application or item you want to use.

If you engage the Zoom feature—another accessibility option—a double tap with three fingers zooms the display.

Flick

If you want to scroll up or down a long list rapidly on your iPod, zip through a selection of album covers in the iPod's Cover Flow view (a view that allows you to browse your music and podcast collection by album cover/artwork), or flip from one photo to another, you use the flick gesture. As you flick faster, the iPod attempts to match your action by scrolling or zipping more rapidly. Slower flicks produce less motion on the display.

To stop the motion initiated by a flick, just place your finger on the display. Motion stops instantly.

Two-finger flick

With the iPod touch 3.0 software, Apple expanded the iPod's gestures to accept multifinger touches. If you download Apple's Remote app from the App Store (Remote is a wonderful application for controlling iTunes remotely on your computer or on Apple TV), you'll find that when you're controlling an Apple TV device, a two-finger flick to the left causes a video playing on Apple TV to back up 10 seconds. I expect that we'll see more of this gesture as the iPod touch matures.

Three-finger flick

As far as I know, the three-finger flick is used only when VoiceOver is on. In that situation, this gesture is used for scrolling.

Drag

For finer control, drag your finger across the display. Use this motion to scroll in a controlled way down a list or email message, or to reposition an enlarged image or Web page. You also drag the iPod's volume slider and playhead when you're in the Music or Videos area.

Three-finger drag

This multifinger gesture works only with the Zoom accessibility feature. When Zoom is on, a three-finger drag moves the screen so that you can see the parts hidden by the zoom.

Rotor

Rotor is another special gesture reserved for when VoiceOver is turned on. You place two fingers on the iPod's screen and turn them as though you're turning a dial. I'll talk more about this gesture when I discuss accessibility in Chapter 2.

Stretch/pinch

To expand an image, such as a photo or Web page, place your thumb and index finger together on the iPod's display and then stretch them apart. To make an image smaller, start with your thumb and finger apart and then pinch them together.

Touch and drag

You use this gesture when you want to change the positions of icons. Tap and hold icons on the Home screen, for example, and they start wiggling, indicating that they can be moved. Touch and drag one of them to move it to a different place, or touch and drag it to the edge of the screen to move it to another Home-screen page. In the Music app's More area, you'll find the option to swap out icons along the bottom of the display by touching and dragging new icons into place. You also touch and drag entries in the On-The-Go playlist to change their positions in the list.

Text Entry and Editing

Taps, pinches, and drags help you navigate the iPod, but they won't compose email messages for you, correct spelling mistakes, or delete ill-considered complaints. The iPod's keyboard and a well-placed finger will do these jobs.

Touch typing

The iPod's virtual keyboard largely matches the configuration of your computer's keyboard. You'll find an alphabetic layout when you open most applications (**Figure 1.3**).

Figure 1.3
The iPod touch's keyboard.

To capitalize characters, tap the up-arrow key (the iPod's Shift key). To view numbers and most punctuation, tap the .?123 key. To see less-used characters (including £, ¥, and €), choose the numbers layout by tapping the .?123 key and then tapping the # + = key. The Space, Return, and Delete keys do exactly what you'd expect. You can produce alternative characters, such as those with accents or umlauts, by tapping and holding the most appropriate character and then waiting for a pop-up menu of characters to appear. Tap and hold the letter *E*, for example, and you get a menu that includes such characters as *è, é, ê,* and *ë.*

To make typing easier, the keyboard's layout changes depending on the application you're using. In Mail, for example, the bottom row holds the @ symbol along with a period (.). Tap and hold that period key, and a pop-up menu displays .net, .edu, .org, and .com; append these extensions simply by sliding your finger over the one you want and then pulling your finger away. While you're working in Safari, the default layout shows period (.), slash (/), and .com keys along the bottom. Tap and hold the .com key to see a pop-up menu that also includes .net, .edu, and .org.

In the bad old days before the iPod touch 3.0 software, only Safari allowed you to type in landscape orientation—providing you a keyboard that offered more space between keys. Now all of Apple's applications that support text input offer landscape orientation. Just turn the iPod on its side, and the screen swivels and displays the broader keyboard.

tip When you type a character, its magnified image appears as you touch it. If you tap the wrong character, leave your finger where it is and slide it to the character you want; the character won't be "typed" until you let go of it.

Editing text

The iPod offers a unique way to edit text. You needn't tap the Delete key time and again to work your way back to your mistake. Instead, tap and hold the line of text you want to edit. When you do, a magnifying glass appears (**Figure 1.4**), showing a close-up view of the area under your finger. Inside this magnified view is a blinking cursor. Drag the cursor to where you want to make your correction—after the word or letter you want to correct—and then press the Delete key to remove the text. In most cases, you can also tap between words to insert the cursor there.

Figure 1.4

Tap and hold to magnify your mistakes.

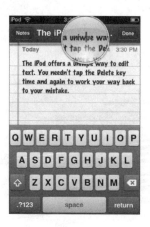

Cut, Copy, and Paste

Let the heavenly trumpets blare: Cut, copy, and paste are now possible with the iPod touch! What's more, they're easy to do.

Editing text

To select text for cutting or pasting in editable text—such as an email message or note—tap where you want to insert a cursor and then tap the cursor that you just inserted. A balloon appears that includes the words *Select, Select All,* and (if you've already copied something) *Paste.* To select the word closest to the cursor, tap Select. To select everything on the page, tap Select All.

When you do either of these things, the balloon changes to display the words *Cut, Copy,* and *Paste;* the text is highlighted in blue; and blue handles appear at the beginning and end of the text (**Figure 1.5** on the following page).

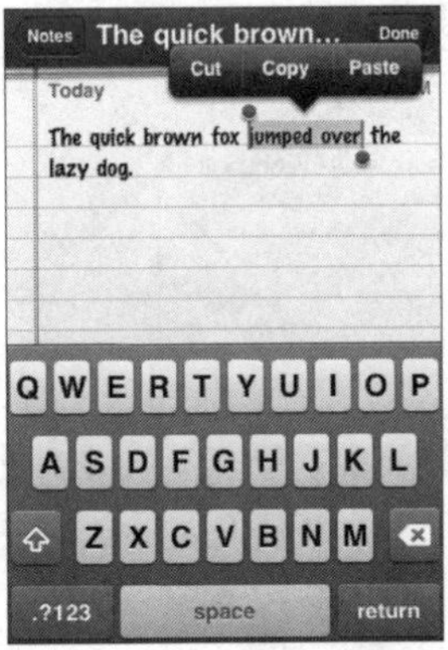

Figure 1.5

With a couple of taps, you can cut, copy, and paste on your iPod touch.

To alter the size of the selection, just drag the handles. When you've selected what you want, tap Cut to make the selected text disappear and add it to the iPod's clipboard (a virtual holding area for storing cut and copied items), Copy to leave the text where it is but also place a copy of it on the clipboard, or Paste to replace the selected text with whatever is currently on the clipboard.

To paste material on the clipboard, just tap somewhere to place the insertion cursor, tap that cursor, and select Paste in the balloon.

If you want to copy *jumped over* from the phrase *The quick brown fox jumped over the lazy dog* in the Notes application, for example, you do this:

1. Tap next to the *j* in *jumped* to insert the cursor.

2. Tap the cursor to select *jumped* and produce the Select, Select All, Paste balloon.

3. Tap Select, and drag the blue handle at the end of *jumped* to the end of the word *over*.

4. With *jumped over* now selected, tap Copy.

Now, to insert the phrase *jumped over* into an email message, do this:

1. Return to the Home screen by clicking the Home button.

2. Tap the Mail application, and create a new email message.

3. Tap to place the cursor in the message.

4. Tap that cursor to produce the Select, Select All, Paste balloon.

5. Tap Paste to insert *jumped over* at the cursor location.

Copying Safari text

You can copy (though not cut) content from Safari as well, even though that text is not editable. Launch Safari, and tap the text you'd like to copy. The magnifying-glass icon appears, and you can choose a selection point. Then, just as you do with text in an email or text message, you can expand the selection and copy it.

tip **If you'd like to copy an entire block of text—a column of text on a Web site, for example—just tap the edge of that block, away from any specific text. Everything in the block is automatically selected, and a Copy balloon appears.**

Once more, here's a real-world example:

You're in a wedding band and preparing for the next client's trip down the aisle. The bride and groom have requested Nirvana's "Smells Like Teen Spirit." The band leader launches Safari, uses Google to search for *Smells Like Teen Spirit lyrics,* and taps one of the many links that produce those lyrics.

On the resulting Web page, she discovers that the lyrics are contained within a block. She taps one of the edges of the block to highlight all the text in the block and then taps Copy to copy it.

Next, she clicks the Home button, taps Mail, creates a new email message, taps in the body of the message to insert the cursor, taps the cursor, and taps Paste in the balloon that appears. The lyrics are pasted into the message. Finally, she addresses the message to the band's singer and sends it.

Copying Safari images

You can also copy images in Safari. To do that, just tap and hold an image. A screen pops up from the bottom of the display, listing either three or five options.

If the image acts as a hyperlink (meaning that when you tap the image, you're taken to a Web page linked to that image), you'll see five buttons: Open, Open in New Page, Save Image, Copy, and Cancel (**Figure 1.6**). Above these buttons is the destination address (or *URL*).

Figure 1.6

Tap and hold a linked image in Safari, and you see these options.

The buttons work this way:

- **Open** takes you to the Web page that's linked to the image.

- **Open in New Page** saves the current page and opens a new browser page in Safari. (I cover this multiple-page Safari stuff in Chapter 6.)

- **Save Image** places a copy of the image in the Photos application.

- **Copy** places on the clipboard a copy of the URL that's linked to the image.

- **Cancel** does exactly what it suggests.

If the image isn't linked to anything but is simply a picture, when you tap it, you see the Save Image, Copy, and Cancel buttons:

- **Save Image** places a copy of the image in the Photos application.

- **Copy** copies the image to the clipboard, thus providing you the opportunity to paste it into an email message.

- **Cancel** does . . . you know.

> **tip** Cut, copy, and paste aren't limited to Notes, Safari, and Mail. You can copy and paste numbers that appear in the Calculator application's results field, for example. Also, because the cut, copy, and paste features are available to anyone who creates iPod touch/iPhone applications, you'll find them used in a variety of apps that you can purchase from the App Store.

2

Setup, Settings, and Sync

As much fun as it is to fondle your new iPod touch (and smudge its shiny silver back in the process), it's time to stop admiring the sheer awesomeness of its design and start doing practical things with it. In this chapter, you do just that.

Setting up the iPod touch

You begin by establishing a relationship between the iPod and iTunes to make the iPod comfortable with your media, email accounts, and personal information.

Get iTunes

iTunes is, in nearly all instances, the conduit for passing information between your computer and the iPod touch. Without it, your iPod will be a pretty limited hunk of technology. Therefore, if you don't have a copy of iTunes 9 or later, now's the time to make a beeline for www.apple.com/itunes/download. (iTunes 9 is the most current version as I write these words, and Apple doesn't include a copy of iTunes in the box.)

iTunes is available in both Macintosh and Windows versions. For the iPod to work with your Mac, you must be running Mac OS X 10.4.11 or later, and your Mac should have a 500 MHz G3 processor or better. PC users must be running Windows XP (with Service Pack 2), Vista, or Windows 7 on a 500 MHz Pentium processor or better.

Plug in the iPod

Plug the included USB cable into a free USB 2.0 port on your Mac or PC. Then plug the data-connector end of the cable into the bottom of the iPod. When you do, iTunes should launch automatically and display the Set Up Your iPod screen. (You may also see a friendly offer to search your iTunes Library for songs that can be turned into ringtones. Feel free to ignore it for now.)

What initially appears on the setup screen with regard to the iPod depends on whether you've previously jacked an iPod touch or iPhone into your computer. If not, you see a Name field containing something like *Joe Blow's iPod touch* and, below that, options titled Automatically

Sync Songs and Videos to My iPod (enabled by default), Automatically
Add Photos to This iPod, and Automatically Sync Applications.

If you've plugged an iPod touch or iPhone into this computer before—
if this iPod is an additional iPod touch or you also own an iPhone—you'll
be offered the opportunity to set up your iPod as a new device or restore
it from a backup of your previous iPod (**Figure 2.1**).

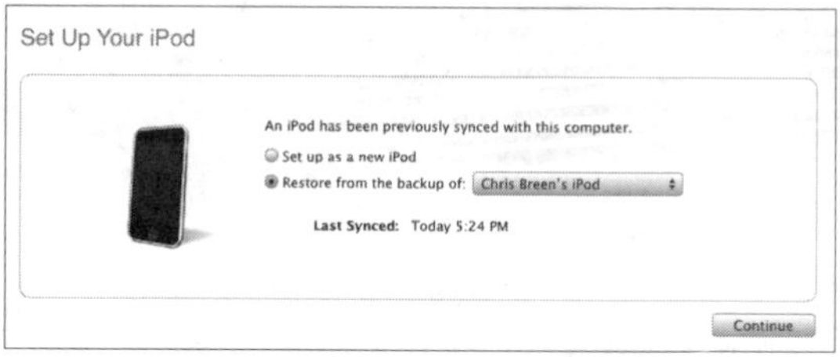

Figure 2.1
*Setting up the
iPod touch.*

To restore your iPod with this old information, simply select the Restore
from the Backup of . . . radio button, click the pop-up menu to the right,
choose the backup you'd like to restore from (the Last Synced entry below
the menu tells you the age of this backup), and then click Continue. The
iPod displays *Restore in Progress* while iTunes restores it with the data
from the backup you selected.

If you'd rather tell iTunes exactly which music and videos to sync,
you can do this later and in a more specific fashion. Simply clear the
Automatically Sync Songs and Videos to My iPod check box in this
window and then click Done.

Your iPod touch and iTunes have engaged in the equivalent of a warm
handshake. I delve into the more intimate details of their relationship
later in this chapter. But first, it's important that you become familiar
with the iPod touch's settings so that you can use them to your advantage when you deal with iTunes.

Configuring the Settings

As its name implies, the Settings screen is where you control much of the iPod touch's behavior (**Figure 2.2**). Here's what you'll see within each setting.

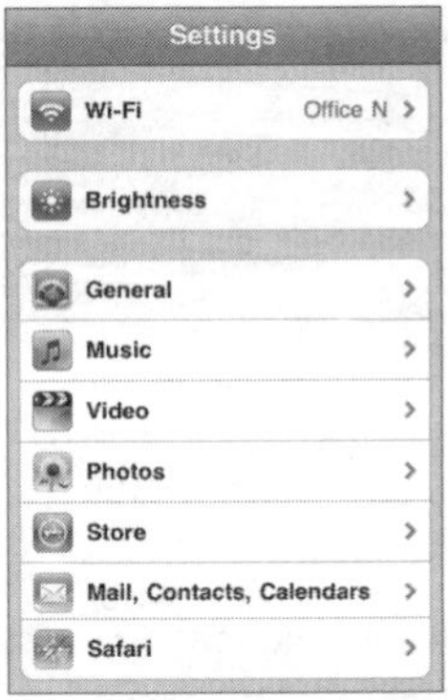

Figure 2.2
Setting up the iPod touch.

Wi-Fi

The iPod touch supports 802.11 wireless networking. In the Wi-Fi Networks screen that appears when you tap Wi-Fi in the Settings screen, you can turn Wi-Fi on or off. Turning it off saves some battery power.

Below this is the Choose a Network area. Any visible Wi-Fi networks within range appear in a list below; those that have a lock icon next to them are password-protected. To access a password-protected network, simply tap its name, enter the password with the keyboard that appears, and tap Join.

To see detailed network information, tap the blue symbol to the right of the network's name. A new screen appears, listing such information as IP Address, Subnet Mask, Router, DNS, Search Domains, and Client ID. At the bottom of one of these screens, you see an HTTP Proxy area with the choices Off, Manual, and Auto. An IT or ISP representative will tell you whether you need to muck with these settings.

Finally, the bottom of the Wi-Fi Networks screen includes the Ask to Join Networks option. Leave this option set on (as it is by default), and your iPod will join known networks automatically and ask to join a network if no known network is available. If you switch the option off, you'll have to join networks manually without being asked. To do so, tap Other; then, using the keyboard that appears, enter the name of the network and password (if required).

Brightness

By default, the iPod's display brightness is adjusted automatically, based on the light it senses around it. When you're outdoors on a sunny day, for example, the screen brightens; when you're inside a dark room, the display dims. If you'd like to override the automatic brightness settings—when you want to save battery power by making the display dimmer than the iPod thinks necessary, for example—you do so in this screen. Turn auto-brightness off and drag the slider to adjust brightness up or down.

General

The General settings are . . . well, pretty general. The grouping consists of a hodgepodge of miscellaneous controls (**Figure 2.3** on the following page).

About

This screen provides your iPod's vital statistics: the number of audio tracks, videos, photos, and applications on the iPod; total capacity; how much storage space remains; software version; serial and model numbers; Wi-Fi and Bluetooth addresses; and a Legal command that, when tapped, leads to a seemingly endless screen of legal mumbo jumbo.

Figure 2.3
*An elongated
view of the
General screen.*

Settings	General	
About		›
Wallpaper		›
Sounds		›
Network		›
Bluetooth	Off	›
Location Services	ON	
Auto-Lock	Never	›
Passcode Lock	Off	›
Restrictions	Off	›
Home		›
Date & Time		›
Keyboard		›
International		›
Accessibility		›
Reset		›

Wallpaper

On the iPod, *wallpaper* refers to an image you choose, which appears
when you unlock the device. To set and adjust your wallpaper picture, tap
the Wallpaper control and then navigate to an image file in the collection
provided by Apple, an image you've taken using the iPod's screen-shot
shortcut (click and hold the Home button, and briefly press the Sleep/
Wake button), or an image you've synced to your iPod via iTunes' Photos
tab. Just tap the image, and the iPod touch shows you a preview of it as
wallpaper (**Figure 2.4**).

Figure 2.4
*Creating a
wallpaper image.*

Sounds

In the Sounds screen (**Figure 2.5**), you can turn alerts on for these events: New Mail, Sent Mail, Calendar Alerts, Lock Sounds, and Keyboard Clicks. Each event has a On/Off toggle switch next to it; you use this switch to make your audio choice. By default, all sounds are switched on. You can use the volume slider at the top of this screen to adjust the volume of the alert sounds. (You can also use the iPod's Volume toggle switch to adjust this slider up or down.)

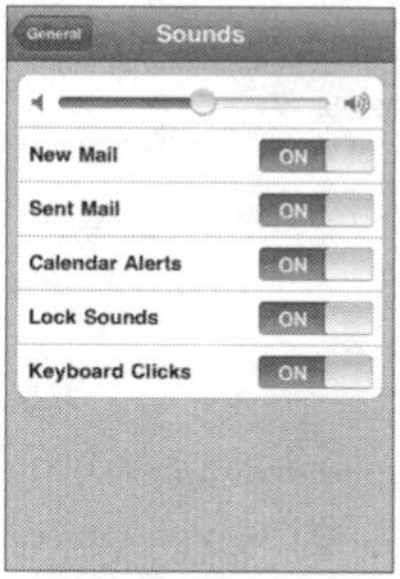

Figure 2.5
The iPod touch's Sounds setting screen.

Network

The Network setting includes options for configuring VPN (virtual private networks) and Wi-Fi.

A *VPN* is an encrypted network protocol, used by many companies, that allows authorized outsiders to join the company network regardless of their locations. When you choose VPN, you're shown the VPN window, which includes a switch for turning VPN on or off; the Choose a Configuration area, which includes any VPN networks you've created; and an Add VPN Configuration button that you tap to view an Add Configuration screen with a list of fields to fill in, including Server,

Account, and Password. You can also choose among L2TP, PPTP, and IPSec networks.

note Configuring a VPN is beyond the mission of this small book. The IT department at your company will be able to tell you how to configure VPN on your iPod touch.

When you tap the Wi-Fi entry in the Network screen, you're taken to the Wi-Fi Networks screen, which I've already discussed.

Bluetooth

This setting is a simple on/off option. When you turn it on, the iPod becomes discoverable and searches for other Bluetooth devices. Turning Bluetooth off can save power. Any Bluetooth devices you've paired your iPod with are listed in the Devices area.

note The iPod touch 3.0 software provided improved Bluetooth support. Now you can use Bluetooth stereo headphones with the iPod touch, for example. You still can't do several other desirable things, however, such as use a Bluetooth keyboard with your iPod, copy files between the iPod and your computer over a Bluetooth connection, or wirelessly sync your iPod over Bluetooth.

Location Services

The iPod is one smart media player. Unlike other such devices, it often knows its location when it's within range of a Wi-Fi network—even if it's not connected to that network. It performs this trick via Wi-Fi location. It works this way:

Some Wi-Fi routers know their geographic coordinates. Those that do will broadcast this information to your iPod touch. Using this information, the iPod can often make a pretty good guess about where it is in relation to those routers based on the strength of their signals. This feature is slick, but it can eat up the iPod touch's battery charge. When you want to conserve power, switch this option off.

Auto-Lock

The iPod equivalent of a keypad lock, Auto-Lock tells the touchscreen to ignore taps after a customizable period of inactivity. Use these controls to specify that interval: 1, 2, 3, 4, or 5 Minutes, or Never. To make the iPod pay attention again after it autolocks, click the Home button.

When the iPod is locked, you can still use the iPod's Volume switch to change the volume while listening to music or placing calls. The button on the headset's mic works when the iPod is locked, too.

Passcode Lock

You'd hate to lose your iPod. Worse, you'd hate to lose your iPod and have some ne'er-do-well dig through it for your email, contacts, and schedule. If you fear that your iPod could fall into the wrong hands (and yes, that may just mean your surly teenage daughter), create a passcode. To do so, tap Passcode Lock; then enter and re-enter a four-digit password with the numeric keypad (**Figure 2.6**).

Figure 2.6
Entering a passcode.

The next screen offers the option to turn the passcode off (useful if you decide that you no longer require a passcode), change it (for . . . well, you know), and a Require Passcode area that offers the options Immediately; After 1, 5, or 15 Minutes; and After 1 or 4 Hours. At the very bottom of the screen is an Erase Data On/Off option. If someone fails to enter the correct passcode after 10 attempts, the iPod's data will be erased.

Restrictions

With the iPod touch 2.0 software came a form of parental controls called *restrictions*. The 3.0 software gave you finer control of the kind of content you get from the iTunes and App stores. Tap Restrictions, and in the top part of the screen labeled Allow, you see options for shutting off Safari, YouTube, iTunes, Installing Apps, and Location. In the Allowed Content area, you can switch off in-application purchases (add-on levels for games, for example), choose ratings for specific countries (Australia, Canada, France, Germany, Ireland, Japan, New Zealand, the United Kingdom, and the United States), disallow playing explicit music and podcasts, select allowed movies by rating (G, PG, PG-13, R, and NC-17), select allowed TV shows (TV-Y, TV-Y7, TV-G, TV-PG, TV-14, and TV-MA), and allow apps by age ratings (4+, 9+, 12+, and 17+). By default, restrictions are turned off, meaning that everything is allowed.

To impose restrictions, first tap Enable Restrictions at the top of the screen. You'll be asked to enter and confirm a four-digit password. When you do, you're allowed to use On/Off switches for functions in the Allow section and for the In-App Purchases option. In the Allowed Content area, you tap one of the entries and then tap the ratings restriction you want to impose (**Figure 2.7**). When you're ready to free all the iPod's functions, tap Disable Restrictions. You'll be asked to enter the restrictions password. When you do, all functionality is restored.

Figure 2.7

Imposing movie restrictions.

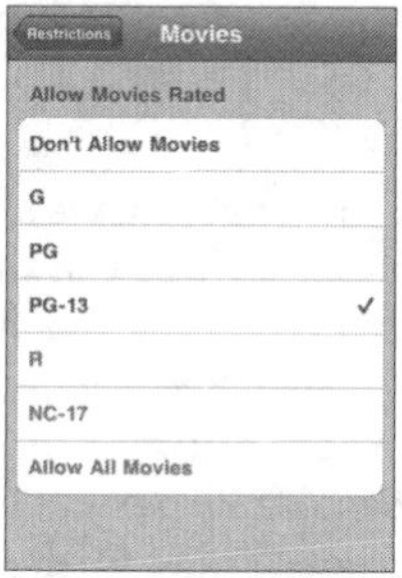

Home

The Home button on the iPod's face can do more than just transport you to the Home screen. In this setting, you determine what happens when you give the Home button two rapid clicks. Options are Home, Search, and iPod.

Below is an iPod Controls switch. When this switch is on, and you're playing music, double-clicking the Home button shows the iPod play-controls overlay, regardless of how you've set the double-click function.

When you're looking at the very first Home page and click the Home button, you move one screen to the left to the Spotlight search screen. See the nearby "Search" sidebar for more information on this feature.

Search

With the iPod touch 3.0 software came ways to search your iPod. The obvious way to search is to visit the first page of the Home screen and swipe your finger to the right to produce the Search screen. (You can also click the Home button once while you're on the first page of the Home screen to produce the Search screen.)

(continued on next page)

Search (continued)

The power of search goes beyond this screen, however; it's spread throughout the iPod touch applications. When you launch the Contacts application, for example, you'll find a Search field at the top of the screen. This same kind of Search field appears in other applications, including Mail, Notes, and Music. In these applications, however, the Search field doesn't appear by default. To produce it, just flick your finger down the screen. The Search field bounces down into view.

You can configure the kind of results you get from the main Search screen by tapping the Search Results entry at the bottom of the Home setting screen (in the General setting). Here, you see a list of items you can search for on your iPod touch (**Figure 2.8**). Search results appear in this order, but you can change that order by dragging items up or down in the list by using the drag handles on the right side of the screen.

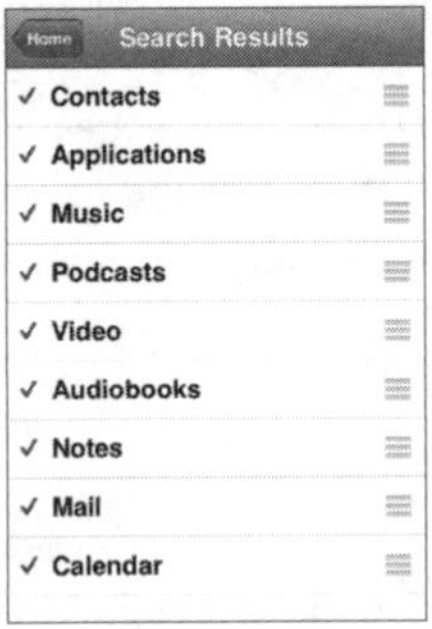

Figure 2.8

Configuring the iPod touch's Search filters.

By default, all these options are enabled. If you don't want certain kinds of items to appear when you search—podcasts and calendar items, for example—just tap them to uncheck them.

Date & Time

The Date & Time settings include a switch for enabling 24-hour time; a Time Zone entry that, when tapped, produces a Time Zone screen, where you can enter a medium-to-large city to establish a time zone; and a Set Date & Time command that, when tapped, takes you to a screen where you can enter the date and time by using a wheel controller (**Figure 2.9**).

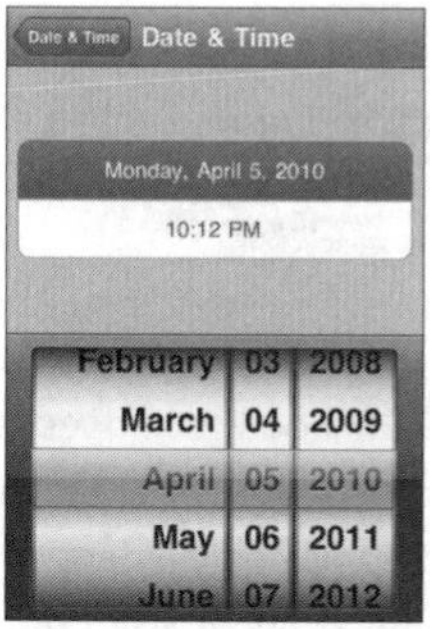

Figure 2.9
Setting the iPod's date and time manually.

Date & Time	Date & Time
Monday, April 5, 2010	
10:12 PM	

February	03	2008
March	04	2009
April	05	2010
May	06	2011
June	07	2012

Keyboard

Are you sensitive enough about your iPod autocorrecting your typing errors that you want to disable that feature? Care to turn autocapitalization on or off (*on* means that the iPod automatically capitalizes words after a period, question mark, or exclamation point)? Or to enable or disable Caps Lock (a feature that types in ALL CAPITALS when you double-tap the keyboard's spacebar)? Or to configure the iPod so that when you tap the spacebar at the end of a sentence, the iPod types a period and adds a space? Here's where you do these things.

Below these four On/Off options, you see International Keyboards. Tap it, and you're taken to a Keyboards screen, where you can switch on additional keyboards. Do so, and when you're using an application that requires the iPod's keyboard, a small globe icon appears to the left of the spacebar. Tap it, and you can switch keyboards. The name of the selected keyboard appears briefly on the spacebar. The number of activated keyboards is reflected next to the International Keyboard entry in the Keyboard screen—*International Keyboards 5*, for example.

International

The International setting is where you choose the language for your iPod, which supports 30 languages, including English, French, Japanese, Chinese, Korean, German, Italian, Portuguese, Romanian, Behasa Indonesian, and Polish.

On the 32 GB and 64 GB iPod touch, you'll see a Voice Control command below the Language entry. (The 8 GB iPod touch doesn't support Voice Control.) Tap this command, and you discover that you can speak to your iPod in one of 21 languages. The iPod not only listens for commands in the language you select, but also tells you what it's doing in a robotic form of that language. VoiceOver, the iPod's screen reader, speaks in the language that you've chosen here.

tip U.S. iPod touch owners who want a tonier-sounding iPod—yet one that still understands their commands—should choose English (United Kingdom) from this list to hear responses delivered in a feminine British accent.

The Keyboards command appears in the International screen as well. Tap it, and you're taken to your old friend the Keyboards screen, where you can enable additional keyboards.

At the bottom of the International screen, you discover the Region Format command. Tap it, and you can choose among a seemingly endless list of countries supported by the iPod touch. Choose a country, and the format for date, time, and telephone number changes.

Accessibility (32 GB and 64 GB iPod touches only)

Apple has taken its world-class VoiceOver technology feature from
Mac OS X and adapted it for the 32 GB and 64 GB iPod touches (as well
as the iPhone). Now the blind and visually impaired can navigate an iPod
touch's touchscreen—something that many people thought would be
impossible—thanks to the voice cues and modified commands offered
on the iPod.

The accessibility feature offers not only the VoiceOver screen reader—
which speaks the name of onscreen elements as well as items under
your finger—but also a Zoom feature for enlarging the screen; a White
on Black toggle that inverts the iPod's screen colors, making it easier for
some visually impaired users to read; Mono Audio, which mixes the left
and right channels of a stereo track into both the left and right earbuds;
and Speak Auto-Text, which alerts the user to autocorrections and capi-
talizations with VoiceOver's voice (**Figure 2.10**). Finally, the Accessibility
setting offers a Home button triple-click feature. The response to a triple
click can be Off, Toggle VoiceOver, Toggle White on Black, or Ask.

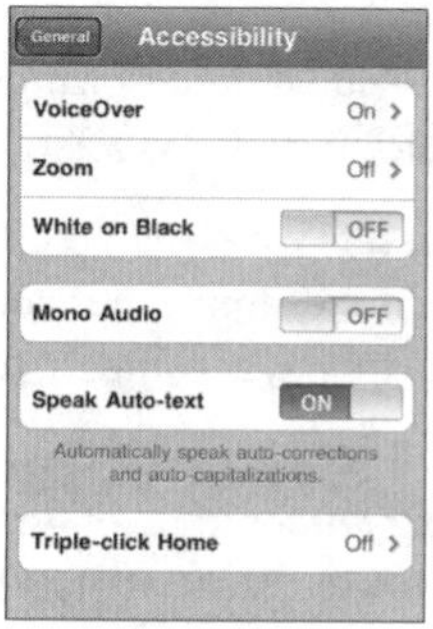

Figure 2.10
*The Accessibility
screen with
VoiceOver on.*

General   Accessibility
VoiceOver	On >
Zoom	Off >
White on Black	OFF
Mono Audio	OFF
Speak Auto-text	ON
Automatically speak auto-corrections and auto-capitalizations.
Triple-click Home	Off >

> **note** You can enable either VoiceOver (the screen reader) or Zoom (which
> does exactly as its name implies), but not both.

When you tap VoiceOver, you have a few options:

- You can activate or deactivate the Speak Hints option, which reads items on a screen to you.

- You can adjust the speaking rate with a slider. (I find the voice too fast in the default setting.)

- You can determine what kind of typing feedback VoiceOver gives you: characters, words, characters and words, or nothing.

VoiceOver isn't difficult to learn, but it takes practice. If you're a Mac user who's familiar with VoiceOver on the Mac, the workings of this feature will be familiar. Selecting letters and typing on a virtual keyboard take some getting used to, however.

All the applications that ship with the iPod are compatible with VoiceOver, and because VoiceOver is built into the operating system, third-party applications take advantage of it as well. The one iPod touch 3.0 software feature that isn't supported by VoiceOver is cut, copy, and paste.

Reset

To remove information from your iPod without syncing it with your computer, you use this screen, which includes a variety of options:

- **Reset All Settings.** This option resets your iPod's preferences (your Network and Keyboard settings, for example) but doesn't delete media or data (your mail settings, bookmarks, or contacts, for example).

- **Erase All Content and Settings.** If your iPod is packed with pirated music, and the Recording Industry Association of America is banging on the door, this option is the one to choose. It erases your preferences and also removes data and media. After you've performed this action, you'll need to sync your iPod with iTunes to put this material back on the device.

- **Reset Network Settings.** Choose this option, and any networks you've used and your VPN settings are erased. Additionally, the iPod switches Wi-Fi on and off, thus disconnecting you from the network you're connected to.

- **Reset Keyboard Dictionary.** As you type on your iPod's keyboard, word suggestions occasionally crop up. This feature is really handy when the iPod guesses the word you're trying to type. If the word is correct, just tap the spacebar, and the word appears complete onscreen. But if the iPod always guesses particular words incorrectly—your last name, for example—you can correct it by tapping the suggestion and continuing to type. The dictionary will learn that word.

When you tap Reset Keyboard Dictionary, the dictionary returns to its original state, and your additions are erased.

- **Reset Home Screen Layout.** You can move icons on the Home screen around by tapping and holding them until they wiggle, at which point you can move them to another position on that screen or move them to a new screen by dragging them to the right or left edge of the iPod's display. When you invoke this command, the icons on the Home screen return to their default locations, and third-party applications are arranged in alphabetical order.

- **Reset Location Warnings.** The iPod will warn you when an application wants to use the iPod's location services. After you OK the warning a second time for a particular application, the iPod no longer issues the warning for that application. To reset the iPod so that it starts asking again, invoke this reset.

note Fear not that a slip of the finger is going to delete your valuable data. The iPod always pops up a panel that asks you to confirm any Reset choice.

And more

The iPod touch includes six more Settings screens by default: Music; Video; Photos; Store; Mail, Contacts, Calendars; and Safari. (In truth, you may see several more, because some third-party applications that you download from the App Store place their settings commands in the Settings screen too.) Because these settings are tied to iPod touch functions, I discuss them in the chapters devoted to those subjects.

Syncing the iPod touch

Although you could pack your iPod touch with nothing but content that you download directly from the iTunes and App Stores, there's a good chance that you'd like some of the music and video files that currently reside in your iTunes Library to find places on your iPod. To make that possible, you must sync your iPod to iTunes.

You do that via the several tabs that appear when you select your iPod touch in iTunes' Source list. Those tabs shake out as follows.

Summary

As its name suggests, the Summary tab provides an overview of your iPod. Here, you find the iPod's name (which you can change by clicking it in iTunes' Source list and entering a new name), its capacity, the software version it's running, and its serial number (**Figure 2.11**).

In the Version portion of the tab, you learn whether your iPod's software is up to date. (You can make sure that you have the latest version by clicking the Check for Update button.) Here, you also find a Restore button for placing a new version of the iPhone software on the device. I revisit this button in Chapter 9.

Figure 2.11
*The Summary
tab.*

The Summary tab provides four or five options, depending on which iPod touch you have. The first, Open iTunes When This iPod Is Attached, does exactly that: It tells iTunes to launch when you plug in your iPod into your computer's powered USB 2.0 port. Unless the Manually Manage Music and Videos option is selected (I'll get to that option very shortly), the iPod will sync automatically when iTunes launches. This setting is carried with the iPod, which means that regardless of which computer you jack the iPod into, it does what this setting instructs.

tip The Devices panel of the iTunes Preferences window contains an option similar to this one: the Prevent iPods and iPhones from Syncing Automatically check box. The option in the Summary tab applies only to an individual iPod touch or iPhone; the iTunes setting applies to all iPod touches and iPhones. When you check Prevent iPods and iPhones from Syncing Automatically, no iPod touch or iPhone connected to the computer will sync until you tell it to.

The second option—Sync Only Checked Songs and Videos—tells the iPod to sync only those checked items in your iTunes Library. If you want greater control of what is planted on your iPod, you can check some songs or videos on a playlist in your iTunes Library but not others. The check boxes appear next to the names of the items—"Love Me Do" and

Casablanca, for example. When this option is turned on, when you sync the iPod, it syncs only the items you've checked.

The third option—Manually Manage Music and Videos—makes it possible to drag content from your iTunes Library to the iPod in iTunes' Source list. You can't do this to add music from another computer's library; the iPod can be synced with the music from only one iTunes Library.

 tip This option is a good one to use when you want to add something to the iPod quickly, without going through the whole syncing rigmarole.

The Hidden Autofill Feature

iTunes provides a sneaky way to fill your iPod touch with music without much forethought. That way is the Autofill feature. It works like this:

1. In the Summary pane, enable the Manually Manage Music option.

2. Click the triangle next to the icon of your iPod in iTunes' Source list to expose the playlists (Music, Podcasts, Audiobooks, and so on).

3. Select the iPod's Music entry (the one that appears just below its name in iTunes' Source list).

4. Whoop for joy when you see three new items at the bottom of the iTunes window: the Autofill From pop-up menu, the Settings button, and the Autofill button.

This is what they do:

Autofill From pop-up menu

As I've already mentioned, you can autofill an iPod from any playlist in iTunes. This pop-up menu is where you choose that playlist. If you want your iPod to be filled from every bit of your music library, just accept the default setting, Music.

The Hidden Autofill Feature (continued)

SETTINGS BUTTON

Click this button, and you discover a few options. The first, Replace All Items When Autofilling, does what it suggests; any music on the iPod is removed and replaced with autofilled music. Leaving this box checked is a good way to help ensure that you get a fresh crop of music the next time you listen to your iPod. It's not such a good choice, however, if you want to keep some selections on the iPod (podcasts, for example) and remove others. The second option, Choose Items Randomly, grabs any old tracks in the selected playlist and biffs them onto your iPod. Leave this option off, and the iPod will be filled with as much of the playlist as will fit, starting with the first track and syncing in order.

The third option, Choose Higher Rated Items More Often, is iTunes' way of giving your iPod more of the music you like. I mean, honestly, what's the use of putting music that you loathe on your iPod? If you haven't thought of a good reason for rating your audio files, now you have one. Assign a rating of four or five stars to your favorite tracks, and those tracks are more likely to be moved to your iPod when this option is enabled.

Finally, at the bottom of this window, you see a slider that reads Reserve Space for Disk Use. The slider below runs from 0 MB to the capacity of your iPod—111.61 GB for a 120 GB iPod classic, for example. With this slider, you designate how much space you're willing to hand over for music storage when autofilling.

AUTOFILL BUTTON

This is the "Go ahead and do it" button. Click it, and iTunes will begin autofilling your music using the playlist and settings you've chosen.

When you check Encrypt iPod Backup, which is the fourth and last option if you have anything but a 32 GB or 64 GB iPod touch released in late 2009, you ask iTunes to back up your iPod and password-protect your data. You might do this with a iPod containing sensitive personal or business information that you back up to your computer.

When you select this option, you'll be prompted to enter and verify a password. Thereafter, your iPod will be backed up completely (even if you just backed it up recently), and the backup will be protected. Should you want to change the password—say, because foreign agents weaseled it out of you by putting ants in your pants—click the Change Password button, enter your old password, and then enter and verify a new password.

tip Encrypting a backup can take iTunes a very long time. You might consider starting this process just before you go to bed. It should be complete when you awaken in the morning.

If you have that late-2009 32 GB or 64 GB iPod touch, you'll also see a Configure Universal Access button at the bottom of the options list. Click it to open a Universal Access window, where you can choose which (if any) of the iPod's accessibility features to switch on (**Figure 2.12**).

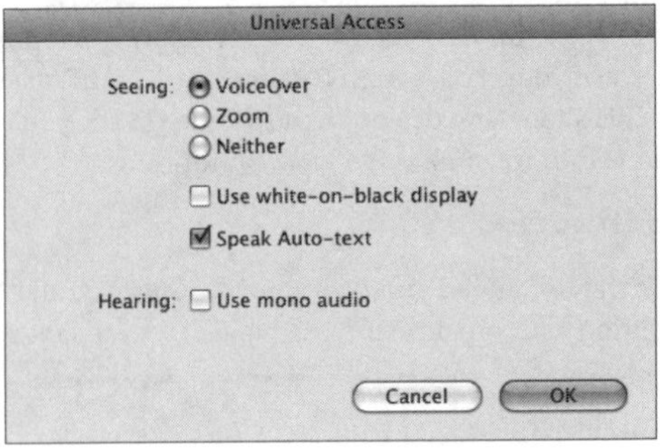

Figure 2.12
Configuring Universal Access.

Down Below

I would be remiss if I left the iPod touch Preferences window without mentioning the Capacity bar at the bottom (**Figure 2.13**). This bar details how your iPod's storage space is being used. Here, you view the total capacity of your iPod, along with statistics for Audio, Video, Photos, Apps, Other (a category that includes contacts, calendars, and applications, for example), and Free (as in free space).

Figure 2.13 *The Capacity bar.*

By default, the amount of storage consumed by a particular item appears below its heading (*Video 1.25 GB,* for example). But if you click the Capacity bar, the statistics labels change—first to the number of items in each category and then, with another click, to the amount of time it would take to play all the videos and audio stored on the iPod (*2.5 days,* for example).

To the right of the Capacity bar is the Sync button. Click this button to sync the iPod right now rather than wait for the next time you dock the thing.

If you make a change in your sync settings—change photo albums, for example, or choose a new movie or podcast to sync—the Sync button disappears, and Cancel and Apply buttons take its place. To sync the iPod immediately with the new settings, click Apply. If you think better of your choices, click Cancel to undo your changes.

Applications

Your iPod touch can use applications sold at Apple's App Store. This tab is where you manage which apps are synced to your iPod. I look at the App Store in greater detail in Chapter 4, but if you'd like to take a look now, here's what you're looking at: All applications that you download from the App Store (either from within iTunes or from an iPod touch or iPhone) are listed in this tab. Those applications that you downloaded from the iPod touch or an iPhone are moved to iTunes only when you sync.

Within this tab, you can choose to sync all applications or just those that you've checked in the list box (**Figure 2.14**). Within this list box, you can sort apps by Name, Category (Books, Games, and Music, for example), or Date. To designate an application for syncing, make sure that the check box next to it is enabled. To search for a particular app, enter its name in the Search field at the top of this tab.

Figure 2.14
The Applications tab.

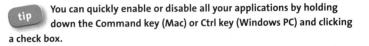

tip You can quickly enable or disable all your applications by holding down the Command key (Mac) or Ctrl key (Windows PC) and clicking a check box.

As you enable applications, you'll see that they appear on the virtual Home screen next to the application list. This Home screen is one of iTunes 9's finest achievements if you have a lot of applications in your iTunes Library. With it, you can easily drag applications to exactly the positions and pages where you'd like them to be. I cover moving apps a little later in the chapter, but for now, know that repositioning them within iTunes is easier than doing it on the iPod.

To move an application, click and drag it to a new position. All applications after it will move up one position. To remove an application, hover your cursor over it until an X appears in its top-left corner; then click the X to remove the application from the iPod touch (but not from your iTunes Library). Although you can change the position of Apple's applications in the Home screen and on the Dock, you can't remove them.

> **tip** The virtual Home screen will always show a blank page (up to 11 pages total). This blank page is helpful because it lets you create new pages for particular kinds of applications. You might use page 2 for social-networking applications such as Twitter and Facebook, pages 3 and 4 for games, and page 5 for productivity applications.

Music

The Music tab (**Figure 2.15** on the following page) contains options for syncing music and music videos to your iPod. With iTunes 9, Apple has completely redone the interface in this and other media windows, making it easier to get exactly the media you want onto your iPod.

Enabling the Sync Music option tells iTunes that you'd like it to sync its music collection to the iPod automatically. If you've enabled the Manually Manage Music and Videos option in the Summary tab, enabling the Sync Music option overrides the Manual option (iTunes will ask you whether you're sure you want to do this). When you've chosen Sync Music, you then have the choice to sync your entire music library or just selected playlists, artists, and genres.

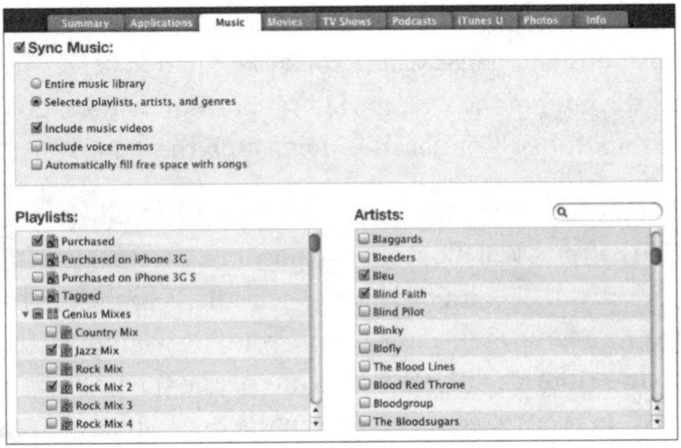

Figure 2.15
The Music pane.

Any songs currently on the iPod that aren't in the iTunes Library or in the selected playlists are erased from the iPod.

Why choose selected playlists, artists, and genres rather than your entire music library? Your iPod may not have the capacity to hold your entire music collection. This option is also a good one to use when several members of your family share an iPod, because it allows you to chunk a music collection into multiple playlists and then rotate those playlists in and out of the iPod.

When you enable the Selected Playlists, Artists, and Genres option, you get three scrolling lists: Playlists, Artists, and Genres.

- **Playlists**

    This list includes all the playlists on your iPod, including Genius Mixes. (I discuss Genius Mixes at greater length in Chapter 3.) For purposes of this discussion, you should understand that if you have a largish music library, a Genius Mix can include as many as 250 tracks. For this reason, you should think carefully about selecting Genius Mixes, as more than a couple could eat up a lot of space on a low-capacity iPod touch.

tip At the top of this list, you'll see Audiobooks with no entries below it, which may lead you to believe that you either have to sync all of your audiobooks or none of them. Enable this option, and you will indeed sync every audiobook that appears in this special playlist. You can sync individual audiobooks, however, by placing them in a separate playlist and then syncing that playlist or by choosing an audiobook's author from the Artists list to the right of the Playlists list.

To sync playlists to your iPod, just enable them in this Playlists list. If you created a folder full of playlists by choosing File > New Playlist Folder and then enabled that folder, all the playlists within the folder will be synced to your iPod.

▪ **Artists**

An improvement that comes with iTunes 9 is the ability to sync individual artists' work to your iPod easily. You do this via the Artists list. Just enable the artists whose music you want to copy to your iPod, and so it shall be when you sync the iPod.

note Notice the Search field above the Artists list. If you have a large iTunes Library, you'll find that this Search feature is a godsend.

▪ **Genres**

Another hat-tip to iTunes 9 for the Genres list. If the holidays are beckoning, and you'd like to add a little musical cheer to the mix, enable the Holiday option in the Genres list, and your iPod will be as full of holiday music as it and your iTunes Library allow. Better yet, when the seemingly endless cheer ends, you can get that stuff off your iPod quickly by unchecking that genre and choosing a less festive genre.

note If you've removed songs from the iTunes Library and want them to remain on your iPod after the update, you'll want to avoid the Selected Playlists, Artists, and Genres option and manage your music manually.

You'll see three additional options in this pane: Include Music Videos, Include Voice Memos, and Automatically Fill Free Space with Songs. Enable the first option, and any music videos in selected playlists will also be synced to your iPod. Turn the option off, and music videos will steer clear, even if they're part of a playlist. Enable the second option, and voice memos that have been copied from your iPod to iTunes can be copied back to your iPod (if you so choose). Switch the option off, and iTunes won't sync voice memos. As for the last option, if you haven't chosen enough music, videos, podcasts, photos, contacts, calendars, and apps to fill your iPod, enabling this option instructs iTunes to top off your iPod with music of its choosing.

Movies

The Movies tab has been rejiggered in iTunes 9 as well. As with the Music tab, you can sync all your movies simply by checking the Sync Movies box and leaving the option below it set to automatically include all movies.

You can add a layer of choice by choosing one of the options from the Automatically Include pop-up menu. These options include syncing the 1, 3, 5, or 10 movies most recently added to iTunes; the 1, 3, 5, or 10 most recent unwatched movies (stuff that you haven't seen and added not all that long ago); or the 1, 3, 5, or 10 least recently unwatched movies (unwatched movies that are starting to gather dust in your iTunes Library).

When you choose one of these options, you're not committed to syncing only those movies. Below, you'll see all the movies in iTunes' Movies playlist with check boxes next to their titles. To sync any of these movies as well, just check their boxes (**Figure 2.16**).

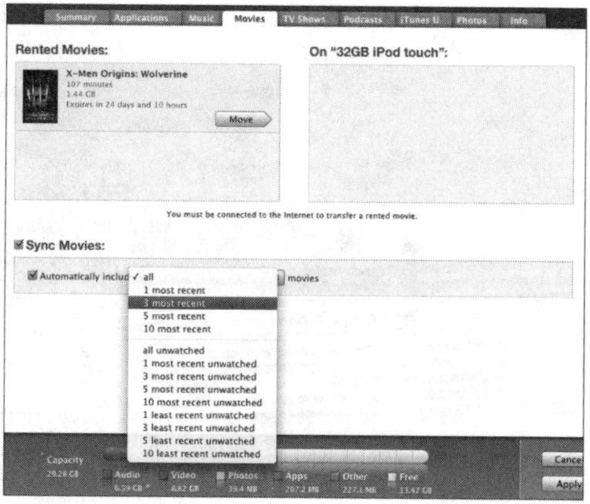

Figure 2.16
The Movies tab.

To be far more particular about the movies that are placed on your iPod, clear the Automatically Include check box. When you do, you see a list of all the movies in iTunes' Movies playlist, plus a list of all the playlists that include movies. Now you can pick just those movies you want, as well as pull movies from playlists you've created that may have a mix of movies and music (such as the Purchased playlist, which contains movies, TV shows, and music that you've bought from the iTunes Store).

Again, if you enable the Sync Movies option, you undo the Manually Manage Movies and Videos setting if you've switched it on.

TV Shows

The TV Shows tab (**Figure 2.17** on the following page) works similarly to the Movies tab. When Sync TV Shows is enabled along with Automatically Include All Episodes of All Shows, all your TV shows will be copied to your iPod when you sync it. But here again, you have the option to sync the 1, 3, 5, or 10 most recent, most recent unwatched, and least recent unwatched episodes of all the shows in your iTunes Library or selected shows.

Figure 2.17
The TV Shows tab.

tip What's with this "least recent unwatched episodes" stuff? If you've
downloaded a season of a TV series, you'd choose this option so that
the shows sync in order from the beginning of the season to the end. If, instead,
you chose the most recent unwatched episodes, playback would start with the
last show and then work its way backward. (If that wouldn't spoil the suspense,
I don't know what would!)

As with the Movies tab, you can clear the Automatically Include check
box, select individual shows and episodes within those shows, and sync
just those shows and episodes to your iPod. Here, too, you'll find a list
that lets you sync shows that are stored within specific playlists.

Podcasts

What puts the *pod* in *podcast* is the iPod. Because people tend to listen to
lots of podcasts, some of which can be long (their files therefore taking
up significant amounts of room), iTunes' Podcasts tab (**Figure 2.18**) lets
you manage which ones are synced to your iPod.

Figure 2.18
The Podcasts tab.

As in each one of these tabs, you have the option to not sync this content, but if you choose to, you have plenty of options. To get it all, just enable Sync Podcasts, and the option below it reads (by default) Automatically Include All Episodes of All Podcasts. If you have a lot of podcast episodes—as many of us do—be choosy by choosing the proper options. Click the All pop-up menu, and you'll see familiar options—1, 3, 5, or 10 most recent; most recent unplayed; and least recent unplayed. Additionally, you'll find options for playing all unplayed; all new; the 1, 3, 5, or 10 most recent new; and the 1, 3, 5, or 10 least recent new. You can do this for all podcasts or just selected podcasts.

Or—and I know you've heard this before—clear the Automatically Include check box, and choose the podcasts and episodes you want to sync. And yes, you can include episodes from podcasts contained within playlists.

Note that video as well as audio podcasts are included here. Because video can consume a lot of storage space, be careful how you choose your video podcasts.

iTunes U

Not terribly long ago, Apple introduced iTunes U, which provides audio and video content from such providers as universities, American Public Media, the Library of Congress, and The Metropolitan Museum of Art. And it's all *free!* Download some of this content, and you'll see that it can be synced very much like podcasts (**Figure 2.19**).

Figure 2.19
The iTunes U tab.

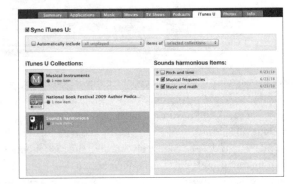

Photos

The Mac and Windows versions of the Photos pane differ slightly. Like so.

Macintosh

If you use a Mac, an iPod with a color display can sync photos with Apple's iPhoto and Aperture, as well as with your Photos folder or a different folder of your choosing. On that Mac, you also have the option to sync all iPhoto albums, events, and faces. Or you can enable the Selected Albums, Events, and Faces, and Automatically Include option (**Figure 2.20**). Do this, and Albums, Events, and Faces lists appear. You can select specific items from these lists, such as all Faces photos that contain a picture of your boyfriend.

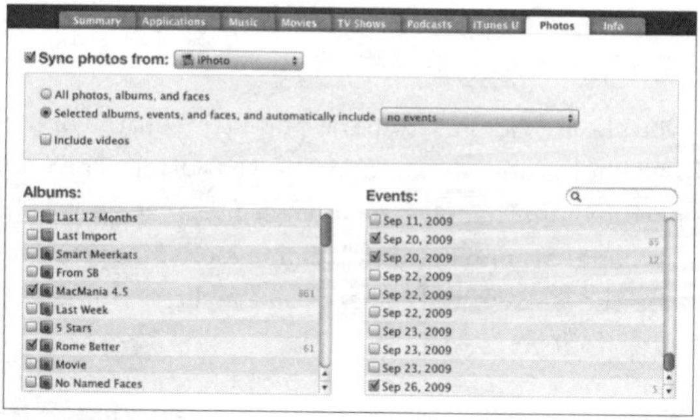

Figure 2.20

The Photos tab in the Mac version of iTunes.

With regard to events, iTunes offers the option to automatically include no events; all events; the most recent, 3, 5, 10, or 20 events; events from the past month; or events from the past 2, 3, 6, or 12 months. If you choose No Events, you can choose the specific events you want on your iPod from the Events list below. iTunes provides a Search field for making these events easier to find.

You also have the option to include videos that have been copied to your iPhoto library—videos you've shot with a pocket camcorder, iPhone, or 5G iPod nano, for example.

Aperture, a tool more often used by pros and advanced photo hobbyists, doesn't enjoy this level of support. Choose Aperture on a Mac version of iTunes, and you see but three options: All Photos and Albums, Selected Albums, and Include Full-Resolution Photos. Choose Selected Albums, and all your Aperture albums appear in a list below. As with iPhoto, you don't have the option to choose individual pictures from albums.

You can also select Choose Folder from the Sync Photos From pop-up menu. When you do, up pops a Change Photos Folder Location navigation window. Just traipse to the folder you want to pull pictures from, and click Open. When you do this, the folder you've chosen appears in the pop-up menu.

If you choose Pictures from this pop-up menu, the options below it change to All Photos and Albums and Selected Folders. The principles of iPhoto/ Aperture import apply here as well. If you choose All Photos, iTunes rummages around in this folder and looks for compatible graphics files. If you choose Selected Folders, you can direct iTunes to look in only those folders that you select.

tip **This method is a good way to copy every picture from your hard drive to your iPod. As far as iTunes is concerned, your hard drive is just another folder. Select it as the source folder with the All Photos option selected, and iTunes grabs all the compatible graphics files it can find, converts them, and plunks them onto your iPod.**

Windows

On a Windows PC, you can sync with your My Pictures folder, a different folder of your choosing, or photo albums created with Adobe Photoshop Elements 3 or later or Adobe Photoshop Album 2 or later. To do this, enable the Sync Photos From option, and from the pop-up menu that follows it, choose the source for your photos.

If you've installed Photoshop Elements (version 3 or later) or Photoshop Album on your PC, the Sync Photos From pop-up menu also contains entries for these programs, allowing you to import pictures from the albums that these programs create.

tip **The tip I propose for copying all the pictures from your Mac to your iPod works in Windows as well. In this case, choose your C drive as the source. When you do, every compatible graphics file will be converted and copied.**

Info

The Info tab is where you choose which data—contacts, calendars, notes, mail accounts, and browser bookmarks—you'd like to sync to your iPod (**Figure 2.21**). This tab is also where you configure iTunes to push email, calendars, contacts, and bookmarks from Apple's MobileMe service to the iPod touch.

Figure 2.21

The Info pane.

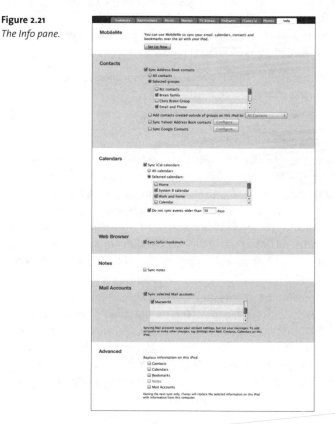

MobileMe

To set up MobileMe, you first have to have a MobileMe account, which costs $100 annually. You can sign up for just such an account at www. apple.com/mobileme. (Apple offers a 60-day free trial if you'd like to test the service before committing.)

Having signed up, click the Set Up Now button in the MobileMe area of the iPod's Info tab. A MobileMe Setup page appears in your default browser. Here, you find links for setting up Macs as well as Windows PCs. Essentially, the steps break down this way:

1. After downloading iTunes 9 or later, sync your contacts, calendars, and bookmarks with your iPod touch.

    You enable these options in the Info tab.

2. Sync your data with MobileMe.

    You do this on a Mac from within the MobileMe system preference. Just choose MobileMe in System Preferences; click the Sync tab; enable the Synchronize with MobileMe option; check the Bookmarks, Calendars, and Contacts boxes in the list box; and click Sync Now. A MobileMe Sync Alert dialog box appears; via a pop-up menu, it lets you Merge All Data, Replace Data on Computer, or Replace All Data on Mobile Me. Choose the setting you want, and click Sync. Your data will be synced.

    On a Windows PC, choose the MobileMe Preferences item in Windows' Control Panels area. (This control panel is installed when you install iTunes 9 or later.) Click the Sync tab, and as you would on a Mac, enable Contacts, Calendars, and Bookmarks. For contacts, you have the option to sync Google, Outlook, Yahoo Address Book, and Windows contacts. Only Outlook calendars are supported. Also, you can sync either Internet Explorer or Safari bookmarks. Just like on the Mac, when you click Sync Now, you see an alert box that offers you the option to merge or replace data.

3. Configure MobileMe on the iPod touch.

Tap the Settings button on the Home screen; tap the Mail, Contacts, Calendars entry; and ensure that Push is set as the Fetch New Data option. If it isn't, tap Fetch New Data, and switch the Push option on in the resulting Fetch New Data screen.

If you haven't yet added your MobileMe account to the iPod, now's the time. Tap Mail, Contacts, Calendars, and in the screen that appears, tap Add Account. In the resulting Add Account screen, tap MobileMe. In the sheet that appears, add your name, MobileMe address (such as *example@me.com*), MobileMe password, and a description of the account (such as *Chris' MobileMe*). Tap Save to add the account.

A MobileMe screen will appear. Here, you can choose those kinds of data—Mail, Contacts, Calendars, and Bookmarks—that you'd like to sync with your iPod touch. Just flick the On/Off slider to On for those bits of information. When everything is set up the way you want it, tap the Mail arrow in the top-left corner of the screen, and your settings will be saved.

And . . . say what? Oh, yes—the Find My iPod touch entry at the bottom of your MobileMe screen. I address that entry fully in Chapter 9, but to help you hold out until then, I'll explain that if you have a MobileMe account, you have the ability to trace your iPod's whereabouts, whether it's hiding under the fridge, resting in the back yard where your dog buried it, or chugging away in the back of a sardine trawler. When you switch on the Find My iPod touch option, this wonder becomes possible. When the option is off, nuh-uh.

The Mail/Entourage Relationship

Although the iPod touch doesn't support pulling account information from Microsoft's popular Macintosh email client, Entourage 2004 and 2008, it can sync Entourage contacts and calendars, but in an indirect way. Recent versions of Entourage include a new Sync Service feature, which you find in Entourage's Preferences window. Choose Sync Services, and you find the option to synchronize contacts with Apple's Address Book and .Mac (now called MobileMe). Likewise, you can synchronize Entourage events and tasks with iCal and MobileMe. (Entourage's Notes, however, are not supported by the iPod touch.) When this option is switched on, Address Book, iCal, and Entourage swap data as you add it.

Enable Sync Services, and any events and contacts you've stored in Entourage are synced to your iPod. Leave it off, and your Entourage data remains missing in action.

Contacts

Here, you find settings for syncing all your contacts or just selected groups that you've created in Address Book (if you use a Mac) or in Windows Address Book, Outlook, Yahoo Address Book, and Google Contacts. (On a Mac, the Yahoo and Google options are listed at the bottom of the Contacts area. Click the Configure button next to either one, agree to the license agreement, and enter your Yahoo or Google user name and password. When this option is enabled, your Yahoo Address Book and Google contacts will make their way to the iPod touch too.)

Below this area, you see the option to put new contacts that you create on the iPod touch in a specific group within Address Book or Outlook. You also see an option for syncing your online Yahoo Address Book and Google contacts.

Calendars

This area works similarly. You can choose to sync all your calendars or, if you're using a Mac, just selected calendars you've created in Apple's iCal (your work calendar, for example, but not your personal calendar). With the iPod touch 2.0 software and later, the iPod displays multiple calendars in its Calendar application. I discuss calendars in greater depth in Chapter 5.

Web Browser

In this area of the Info window in the Macintosh version of iTunes, you'll find a Sync Safari Bookmarks check box. On a Windows PC, a pop-up menu provides the option to sync Safari or Internet Explorer bookmarks.

Notes

Notes is an on/off option. Enable Sync Notes in the Mac version of iTunes, and any notes created on the iPod touch will be synced to the Notes area of Mail—Apple's email client. Likewise, if you create a note in Mail and have this option enabled, that note will be synced to your iPod.) On a Windows PC, notes are be synced to Outlook (and vice versa here, too). I take a closer look at Notes in Chapter 8.

Mail Accounts

iTunes looks for email account settings in Mail on a Mac and in Outlook, Microsoft Mail, and Outlook Express on a Windows PC. (It looks for the settings only; syncing mail accounts doesn't sync messages.) The settings that it finds appear in a list in the Mail Accounts area of the Info tab. You have the option to select the email account(s) you'd like to access with the iPod touch.

tip   If, after allowing iTunes to add email accounts to the Info tab automatically, you add a different account (maybe you've changed Internet
service providers or taken on a MobileMe account, for example), iTunes will add
the account to the Mail Accounts area automatically when you next sync
your iPod.

Advanced

Finally, the Advanced area offers a nifty little workaround when you
plug your iPod touch into another computer. For this feature to work,
you must first choose at least one option above—say, Sync Address Book
Contacts—and then choose the options you want in that area (choose to
sync a specific group of contacts, for example). Now enable the related
option in the Advanced area (you'd choose Contacts if you enabled Sync
Address Book Contacts). When you click the Apply button in the bottom-
right corner of the window, iTunes overwrites the selected information
that's currently on the iPod with the information stored on the computer
to which the iPod is connected.

Note the word *overwrite*. If you do this, the information you had on the
iPod is deleted.

3

iPod touch As iPod

Sure, your iPod touch is a handy device for surfing the Web, grabbing your email, and discovering just how much you've lost in the stock market in a given day. But the word *iPod* appears in its name for good reason. Multitalented though this iPod may be, it's also a heck of a great media player. This chapter focuses on the iPod touch's media capabilities and shows you how to make the most of them.

Getting the Goods

"Eep!" I hear you squeep. "I've never used iTunes or owned an iPod. I have no idea how to get music into iTunes, much less put it on my portable music player. What do I do?"

Relax. I'm not going to tell you how to put your music and movies on your iPod touch until you know how to assemble a music and movie library.

I'll start with music. You have three ways to get tunes into iTunes:

- Recording (or *ripping*, in today's terminology) an audio CD

- Importing music that doesn't come directly from a CD (such as an audio track you downloaded or created in an audio application on your computer)

- Purchasing music from an online emporium such as Apple's iTunes Store

The following sections tell you how to use the first two methods. The iTunes Store is a special-enough place that I discuss it in Chapter 4.

note **The procedures for adding movies and videos are similar, except that iTunes offers no option for ripping DVDs. You can do that, but the procedure is more complicated than ripping an audio CD. I cover ripping DVDs in the following section.**

Rip a CD

Apple intended the process of converting audio-CD music to computer data to be painless, and it is. Here's how to go about it:

1. Launch iTunes.

2. Insert an audio CD into your computer's CD or DVD drive.

By default, iTunes tries to identify the CD you've inserted. It logs on to the Web to download the CD's track information—a very handy feature for those who find typing such minutia to be tedious.

The CD appears in iTunes' Source list under the Devices heading, and the track info appears in the Song list to the right (**Figure 3.1**).

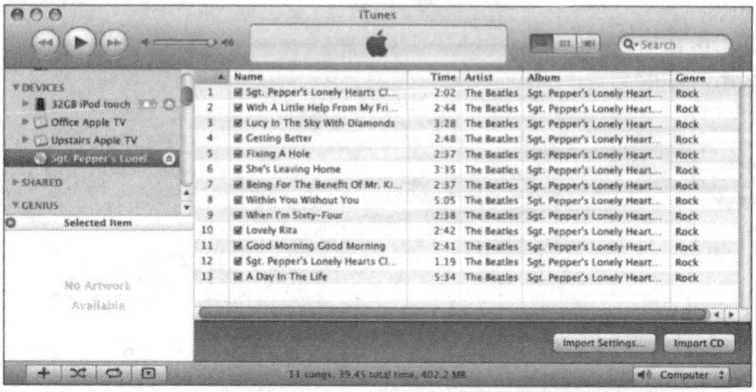

Figure 3.1
A selected CD and its tracks.

Then iTunes displays a dialog box, asking whether you'd like to import the tracks from the CD into your iTunes Library.

3. Click Yes, and iTunes imports the songs; click No, and it doesn't.

> **note** You can change this behavior in iTunes' Preferences window. In the General preference, you find a When You Insert a CD pop-up menu. Make a choice from that menu to direct iTunes to show the CD, begin playing it, ask to import it (the default), import it without asking, or import and then eject it.

4. If you decided earlier not to import the audio but want to do so now, simply select the CD in the Source list and click the Import CD button in the bottom-right corner of the iTunes window.

iTunes begins encoding the files via the method chosen in the Import Settings window (**Figure 3.2** on the following page), which you access by opening iTunes' Preferences window (choose iTunes > Preferences on a Mac or Edit > Preferences on a Windows PC), clicking the General tab, and clicking the Import Settings button. By default, iTunes imports songs in iTunes Plus AAC format at 256 Kbps. (For more on encoding methods, see the sidebar "Import Business: File Formats and Bit Rates" in the next section.)

Figure 3.2
Importing a CD with iTunes.

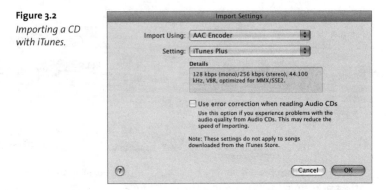

 To import only certain songs, uncheck the boxes next to the titles of songs you don't want to import; then click the Import CD button.

5. Click the Music entry in the Source list.

   You'll find the songs you just imported somewhere in the list.

6. To listen to a song, click its name in the list and then click the Play icon or press the spacebar.

Move music into iTunes

Ripping CDs isn't the only way to put music files on your computer. Suppose that you've downloaded some audio files from the Web and want to put them in iTunes. You have three ways to do that:

- In iTunes, choose File > Add to Library.

  When you choose this command, the Add To Library dialog box appears (**Figure 3.3**). Navigate to the file, folder, or volume you want to add to iTunes, and click Open. iTunes determines which files it thinks it can play and adds them to the library.

Figure 3.3

Navigate to tracks you want to add to iTunes via the Add To Library dialog box.

Combining CD Tracks

There may be occasions when you don't want iTunes to extract individual tracks from a CD, such as when you have a long audiobook that's stored on multiple CDs, and each CD has a dozen or more individual files that represent portions of chapters. Managing what may turn out to be dozens of chapters on an iPod is anything but convenient. To work around a problem like this one, you can combine all the tracks on the CD into a single long track.

To do that, insert the CD, turn down iTunes' offer to rip the CD for you, select the CD in iTunes' Source list, select all the tracks on the CD, and choose Advanced > Join CD Tracks. The contents of the CD will be ripped as one long file.

- Drag files, folders, or entire volumes to the iTunes icon in Mac OS X's Dock, the iTunes icon in Windows' Start menu (if you've pinned iTunes to this menu), or the iTunes icon in either operating system (at which point iTunes launches and adds the dragged files to its library).

- Drag files, folders, or entire volumes into iTunes' main window or the Library entry in the Source list.

  In the Mac versions of iTunes, by default you'll find songs in the iTunes Music folder within the iTunes folder inside the Music folder inside your Mac OS X user folder. The path to my iTunes music files, for example, would be chris/Music/iTunes/iTunes Music.

  Windows users will find their iTunes Music folder by following this path: *yourusername*/My Music (XP) or Music (Vista and Windows 7)/iTunes/iTunes Music.

You can use the same methods to add compatible videos and movies to your iTunes Library. (For more on what makes those videos compatible, see the sidebar "Working with Supported Video Formats" later in the chapter.) Those videos will most likely appear in the Movies playlist in the Source list.

I say *most likely* because there are a few exceptions: Videos specifically designated as music videos appear in the Music playlist, videos designated as TV shows appear in the TV Shows playlist, and video podcasts are filed under Podcasts in iTunes' Source list. See the sidebar "Tag, You're It" later in this chapter for information on how to apply those video designations.

Import Business: File Formats and Bit Rates

MP3, MPEG-4, AAC, AIFF, WAV . . . is the computer industry incapable of speaking plain English?

It may seem so, given the plethora of acronyms floating through modern-day Technotopia. But the lingo and the basics behind it aren't terribly difficult to understand.

MP3, AAC, AIFF, and WAV are audio file formats. The compression methods used to create MP3 and AAC files are termed *lossy* because their encoders remove information from the source sound file to create these smaller files. Fortunately, these encoders are designed to remove the information you're least likely to miss—audio frequencies that humans can't hear easily, for example.

AIFF and WAV files are uncompressed, which means that they contain all the data in the source audio file. When a Macintosh pulls audio from an audio CD, it does so in AIFF format, which is the native uncompressed audio format used by Apple's QuickTime technology. WAV is an AIFF variant used extensively with the Windows operating system.

iTunes supports one other compression format: Apple Lossless. This format is termed a *lossless* encoder because it shrinks files by removing redundant data without discarding any portion of the audio spectrum. This scheme yields sound files with all the audio quality of the source files at around half their size. iTunes and the iPod also support the H.264 and MPEG-4 video formats. These, too, are compressed formats that allow you to fit a great big movie on a tiny iPod.

Now that you're familiar with these file formats, I'll touch on resolution as it applies to audio and video files.

You probably know that the more pixels per inch a digital photograph has, the crisper the image (and the larger the file). Resolution

(continued on next page)

Import Business:
File Formats and Bit Rates (continued)

applies to audio as well. But audio defines resolution by the number of kilobits per second (Kbps) contained in an audio file. *With files encoded similarly*, the higher the kilobit rate, the better-sounding the file (and the larger the file).

I emphasize *with files encoded similarly* because the quality of the file depends a great deal on the encoder used to compress it. Many people claim that if you encode a file at 128 Kbps in both the MP3 and AAC formats, the AAC file sounds better.

The Import Settings menu (which you reach by clicking the Import Settings button within iTunes' General preferences) lets you choose to import files in AAC, AIFF, Apple Lossless, MP3, or WAV format. The Setting pop-up menu is where you choose the resolution of the AAC and MP3 files encoded by iTunes by choosing Custom from the menu. iTunes' default setting is iTunes Plus (256 Kbps). To change this setting, choose High Quality (128 Kbps) or Custom from the Setting pop-up menu. (Spoken Podcast is another option when you choose the AAC Encoder, but it produces quality that's good only for spoken-word audio.) If you choose Custom, the AAC Encoder dialog box appears. Choose a different setting—in a range from 16 Kbps to 320 Kbps—from the Stereo Bit Rate pop-up menu (**Figure 3.4**). Files encoded at a high bit rate sound better than those encoded at a low bit rate (such as 96 Kbps). But files encoded at higher bit rates also take up more space on your hard drive and iPod.

The preset options for MP3 importing include Good Quality (128 Kbps), High Quality (160 Kbps), and Higher Quality (192 Kbps). If you don't care to use one of these settings, choose Custom from this same pop-up menu. In the MP3 Encoder dialog box that appears, you have the option to choose a bit rate ranging from 16 Kbps to 320 Kbps.

Import Business:
File Formats and Bit Rates (continued)

Figure 3.4
*The Stereo Bit
Rate pop-up
menu.*

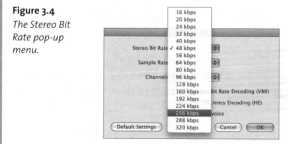

Resolution is important for video as well. Fortunately, iTunes allows
you to convert video to only two formats: iPod/iPhone–compatible
format and Apple TV format. You do this by choosing Advanced >
Create iPod or iPhone Version or Create Apple TV Version, respectively.
These commands provide no tools for adjusting resolution settings.

Creating and Configuring a Playlist

Before you put any media files (music or video) on your iPod, organize
them in iTunes. Doing so will make it far easier to find the media you
want, both on your computer and on your iPod. The best way to organize
that material is through playlists.

A *playlist* is simply a set of tracks and/or videos that you believe should
be grouped in a list. The organizing principle is completely up to you.
You can organize songs by artist, by mood, by style, by song length . . .
heck, if you like, you can have iTunes automatically gather all your 1950s
polka tunes with the letter *z* in their titles. Similarly, you can organize

your videos by criteria including director, actor, and TV-series title. You can mix videos and music tracks within playlists as well, combining, say, music videos and music tracks by the same artist. As far as playlists are concerned, you're the boss.

The following sections look at ways to create playlists.

Standard playlists

Standard playlists are those that you make by hand, selecting each of the media files you want grouped. To create a standard playlist in iTunes, follow these steps:

1. Click the large plus (+) icon in the bottom-left corner of the iTunes window, or choose File > New Playlist (Command-N on the Mac, Ctrl+N in Windows).

2. In the highlighted field that appears next to that new playlist in the Source list, type a name for your new playlist.

3. Click an appropriate entry in the Source list—Music, Movies, TV Shows, or Podcasts—and select the tracks or videos you want to place in the playlist you created.

4. Drag the selected tracks or videos to the new playlist's icon.

5. Arrange the order of the tracks or videos in your new playlist.

   To do this, click the Number column in the main window, and drag tracks up and down in the list. When the iPod is synchronized with iTunes, this order is how the songs will appear in the playlist on your iPod.

   If the songs in your playlist come from the same album, and you want the songs in the playlist to appear in the same order as they do on the original album, click the Album heading.

Playlist from selection

You can also create a new playlist from selected items by following these steps:

1. Command-click (Mac) or Ctrl+click (Windows) songs or videos to select the files you'd like to appear in the new playlist.

2. Choose File > New Playlist from Selection (Command-Shift-N on a Mac, Ctrl+Shift+N on a Windows PC).

   A new playlist containing the selected items will appear under the Playlists heading in the iTunes Source list. If all selected tracks are from the same album, the list will bear the name of the artist and album. If the tracks are from different albums by the same artist, the playlist will be named after the artist. If you've mixed tracks from different artists or combined music with videos, the new playlist will display the name *untitled playlist*.

3. To name (or rename) the playlist, type in the highlighted field.

Smart Playlists

Smart Playlists are slightly different beasts. They include tracks that meet certain conditions you've defined—for example, Fountains of Wayne tracks encoded in AAC format that are shorter than 4 minutes. Here's how to work the magic of a basic Smart Playlist:

1. In iTunes, choose File > New Smart Playlist (Command-Option-N on the Mac, Ctrl+Alt+N in Windows).

   You can also hold down the Option key on the Mac or the Shift key on a Windows PC and then click the gear icon that replaces the plus (+) icon at the bottom of the iTunes window.

2. Choose your criteria.

You'll spy a pop-up menu that allows you to select items by various criteria—including artist, composer, genre, podcast, bit rate, comment, date added, and last played—followed by a Contains field. To choose all songs by Elvis Presley and Elvis Costello, for example, you'd choose Artist from the pop-up menu and then enter **Elvis** in the Contains field (**Figure 3.5**).

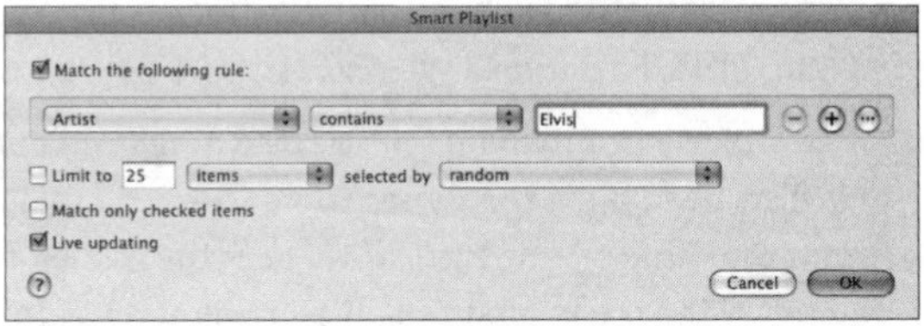

Figure 3.5
The inner workings of a simple Smart Playlist.

You can limit the selections that appear in the playlist by minutes, hours, megabytes, gigabytes, or number of songs. You may want the playlist to contain no more than 2 GB worth of songs and videos, for example.

You'll also see a Live Updating option. When it's switched on, this option ensures that if you add to iTunes any songs or videos that meet the criteria you've set, those files will be added to the playlist. If you add a new Elvis Costello album to iTunes, for example, iTunes updates your Elvis Smart Playlist automatically.

3. Click OK.

A new playlist that contains your smart selections appears in iTunes' Source list.

You don't have to settle for a single criterion. By clicking the plus icon next to a criterion field, you can add other conditions. You could create a playlist containing, say, only songs you've never listened to by punk artists whose names contain the letter *J*.

Conditional Smart Playlists

With iTunes 9, you can create more powerful Smart Playlists than you could before, thanks to a new feature called *nested conditional rules*. With nested conditional rules, you have sets and subsets of rules that can act on previous rules. Perhaps you want a Smart Playlist that picks out music and music-video files that are less than 4 minutes long, that were recorded before 1990, and that fall within the Pop and Soul genres. It would be difficult to get this level of detail in a traditional Smart Playlist—but not quite so difficult in a Smart Playlist that contains nested conditional rules. **Figure 3.6** shows settings for an example conditional Smart Playlist.

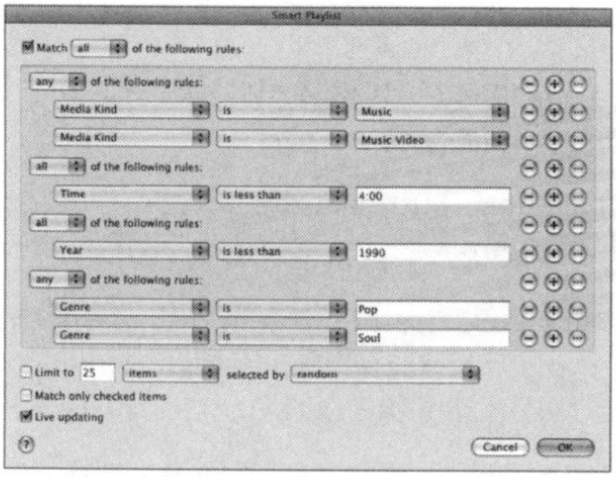

Figure 3.6
A conditional Smart Playlist.

A good way to see how to use nested conditional rules is to duplicate the settings in Figure 3.6. (Later, you can follow this same procedure but choose different settings for your own conditional Smart Playlists.) Follow these steps:

1. In iTunes, choose File > New Smart Playlist (Command-Option-N on the Mac, Ctrl-Alt-N in Windows).

2. In the resulting Smart Playlist window, click the ellipsis (...) button to expand the window.

(continued on next page)

Conditional Smart Playlists (continued)

3. Click the minus (–) button to remove the top condition, which reads (over the pop-up menu) *Artist Contains*.

   For nesting to work properly, you need to start with a conditional, and that first default entry prevents you from doing that.

4. Click the plus (+) button next to *Artist Contains* to create another condition. Configure the two conditions to read *Media Kind is Music* and *Media Kind is Music Video*.

5. In the *All of the Following Rules* section above these two conditions, choose *Any* from the pop-up menu so that it reads *Any of the Following Rules*.

   This setting ensures that the playlist will look for both music and music-video files.

6. Click the ellipsis button at the top of the window to add another condition group.

   If you click the ellipsis button next to one of the Media Kind entries, you'll set a condition that affects only that Media Kind rule. You want something that affects all chosen files.

7. In the new condition group, create a rule that reads *Time is Less Than 4:00*.

   That takes care of the time limit.

8. Click the top ellipsis button again, and create a rule that reads *Year is Less Than 1990*.

   So much for the date.

9. Click the top ellipsis button just one more time to create one last group.

Conditional Smart Playlists (continued)

10. In this group, add two genre conditions that read *Genre is Pop* and *Genre is Soul*.

11. Above these Genre entries, change *All of the Following Rules* to *Any of the Following Rules*.

    Changing *All* to *Any* instructs the playlist to look for any tracks that meet the previous conditions and that are tagged with any of these two genres.

Folders for playlists

You can also file playlists in folders. By invoking the File > New Playlist Folder command, you can lump a bunch of playlists into a single folder. Folders are a great way to keep your playlists separate from your spouse's or to gather groups of similar playlists (All My Jazz Playlists, for example) when you listen to music in iTunes. Regrettably, the iPod touch doesn't respect folders. When you copy a folder that contains playlists to your iPod touch, all the music in that folder is placed in a single playlist on the touch.

Genius playlists and Mixes

With iTunes 8, Apple introduced the compelling Genius feature. When you turn on Genius, you voluntarily (and anonymously) submit the contents of your iTunes Library to Apple. In exchange, Apple analyzes that content and sends a database file of related music in your library back to your computer. Using this file, Genius can create playlists of music that it believes will work well with a track that you've selected.

Say that you select The Rolling Stones' "19th Nervous Breakdown" as the source track in iTunes and then click the Genius icon at the bottom of the iTunes window. Genius creates a playlist of 25 tracks that includes classic rock tracks from your iTunes Library—Donovan's "Mellow Yellow," The Allman Brothers' "Whipping Post," and Deep Purple's "Hush," for example.

In addition to Genius playlists, iTunes 9 can create *Genius Mixes,* which are 250-track playlists chosen by genre from your iTunes Library. In the following sections, I look at the ins and outs of each feature.

Genius playlists

To create Genius playlists with iTunes, follow these steps:

1. Switch on the Genius feature.

   When you install iTunes, you're offered the choice to turn Genius on. Doing so requires an iTunes account. If you don't have one, no worries; when you start the Genius process, you'll find an option for signing up for an account. If you neglected to turn on Genius, you can do so by choosing Store > Turn on Genius. If you're connected to the Internet, iTunes will ask you to sign into your iTunes account.

2. Wait while iTunes configures Genius.

   iTunes gathers information about your music library—specifically, the songs it contains—and sends that information to Apple's servers anonymously. That information is compared with similar data from other users and placed in a database. A database file that contains the relationship data is sent back to your computer.

3. Create a Genius playlist.

   Select a track in your iTunes Library, and click the Genius button in the bottom-right corner of the iTunes window. iTunes will create a new playlist of 25 songs (by default) that should go well with the track you selected. You can ask Genius to create a longer version of this playlist by making a larger choice from the Limit To pop-up menu at the bottom of the window; your choices are 25, 50, 75, and 100 songs. You can also click Refresh to ask Genius to try again.

4. Save the playlist.

When you click the Save Playlist button at the top of the window, iTunes creates a playlist named after your source track—*A Common Disaster*, for example. You can return to any Genius playlist you've created and change the Limit To settings as well as refresh the playlist.

5. Expose the Genius sidebar.

Click the Sidebar icon in the bottom-right corner of the iTunes window to display the Genius sidebar, which is designed to recommend related music from the iTunes Store (**Figure 3.7**).

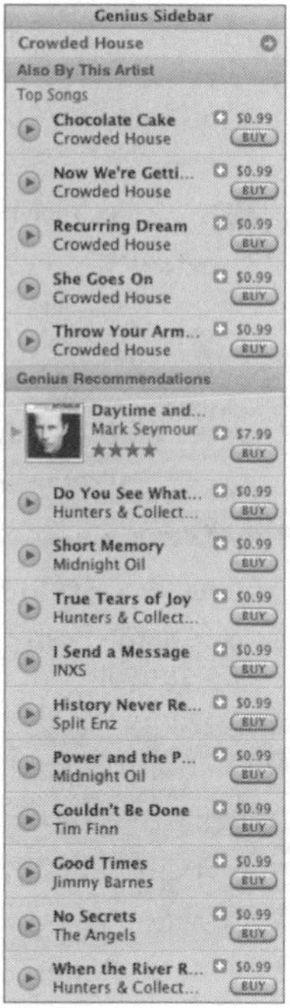

At the top of the sidebar, you'll find entries that include the name of the artist, Also By This Artist (which includes Top Albums and Top Songs entries), and Genius Recommendations. You might also see an iTunes Essentials entry. A small arrow icon next to an entry indicates a

Figure 3.7
The Genius sidebar.

potential trip to the iTunes Store. Click an artist's name, for example, and you'll be taken to the Store page devoted to that artist. Click the arrow icon next to Genius Recommendations, and iTunes creates a list of those recommendations (though this looks like a playlist, you can't save it as such).

Next to the song selections, you'll see both a Preview button (denoted by a small Play icon) and a Buy button. To audition 30 seconds of a track, just click the Preview button. If you like what you've heard and would like to own the track, click Buy. In the resulting dialog box, you'll be prompted for your Apple ID and password. Enter that info and click the Buy button, and the track downloads to your computer.

note You can sync Genius playlists to your iPod just as you can any other playlists.

Genius Mixes

Genius Mixes are new in iTunes 9 and, as I write this chapter, supported only by 2G iPod touches (including the iPod touches released in late 2009), the 5G iPod nano, and the iPhone. Genius Mixes are broader tools than Genius playlists in that they're created based on genres—Rock, Jazz, and Classical, for example.

The "genius" of Genius Mixes is that their content is still related, much like the content of Genius playlists. Unless you have a small music library, it's unlikely that iTunes will produce a Genius Mix including AC/DC, Donovan, Sheryl Crow, and Ry Cooder, even though all four artists may have had a Rock genre tag applied to them. Instead, you may have one Rock Genius Mix that includes '60s artists such as Janis Joplin, Cream, Jimi Hendrix, and The Small Faces. Another Genius Mix could include modern pop artists such as Death Cab for Cutie, The Finn Brothers, The Apples in Stereo, and Feist. So thanks to the enormous database of related music first created when the Genius feature was introduced with iTunes 8, iTunes has the power to create these large mixes that make sense.

Creating them is really easy:

1. Launch iTunes 9 or later.

2. Click the Genius Mixes entry located under the Genius heading in iTunes' Source list.

3. There is no step 3.

iTunes will create up to 12 Genius Mixes. Each Genius Mix is represented by an album cover that, in turn, features four album covers taken from the music in that Genius Mix (**Figure 3.8**). An example Rock Genius Mix, then, could include artwork from Coldplay, Radiohead, Oasis, and John Mayer albums.

Figure 3.8
Genius Mixes.

Unlike Genius playlists, Genius Mixes can't be edited. In fact, you can't even see the contents of one of these mixes. What iTunes provides is exactly what you get. To play one, just click its icon, and the first track in the mix plays. To skip to the next track, click the Next button in iTunes' play controls (located in the top-left corner of the iTunes window) or press your keyboard's right-arrow key.

To sync Genius Mixes, do this:

1. Select your iPod in iTunes' Source list.

2. Click the Music tab.

3. Enable the Sync Music option.

4. Enable the Selected Playlists, Artists, and Genres option.

5. In the Playlists column, look for the Genius Mixes entry; then select all of these mixes (by checking the Genius Mixes check box) or specific mixes (**Figure 3.9**).

Figure 3.9
Selecting Genius Mixes.

6. Sync the iPod.

When you sync a Genius Mix to your iPod touch, a new Genius icon appears at the bottom of the Music-application screen. Tap Genius, and you can select the Genius Mixes on the iPod and play them simply by tapping the Play icon in the center of the screen.

> **tip** If you choose to sync all your music with the iPod, Genius Mixes will be included automatically. If you don't have enough room on the iPod to sync your entire music library, however, Genius Mixes won't be added—which makes sense, as each Genius Mix can include up to 250 tracks.

Configuring iTunes

Intuitive though it may be, iTunes packs a lot of features and power—enough that I could write an entire book about just this application. I have bigger fish to fry: showing you how to get the most out of your iPod. But part of frying those fish is introducing the key iTunes features that can make using and listening to your iPod more enjoyable. In this section, I examine those features.

Setting iTunes preferences

Choose iTunes > Preferences on a Mac or Edit > Preferences on a Windows PC, and you open iTunes' Preferences window. Some of the tabs within this window lead to settings that you should know about.

General

I've already mentioned that within the General preference, you specify what happens when you insert a CD. Elsewhere in this tab, you find options for showing or hiding certain items in iTunes' Source list, including Movies, TV Shows, Podcasts, iTunes U, Audiobooks, Applications, Ringtones, Radio, iTunes DJ, and Genius. If you find iTunes' interface too cluttered, disabling the items you don't use will clean things up.

One of iTunes' most important features is hidden behind the Import Settings button in the General preference. Click Import Settings to open the window of the same name, and you find iTunes' encoder settings— the settings you configure to determine which codec iTunes uses to rip CDs and convert audio files, as well as what bit rates the encoder uses. I explain the workings of encoders and bit rates earlier in this chapter, in the "Import Business: File Formats and Bit Rates" sidebar.

tip **The Import Settings window also includes the Use Error Correction When Reading Audio CDs option. If you're having difficulty ripping an audio CD (because it's dirty, for example), enable this option. iTunes will try that much harder to rip the CD properly, though the process will take longer.**

Playback

Here, you can determine where in the iTunes interface movies, TV shows, and music videos are displayed (in a separate window, for example) and set the default and subtitle languages for movies. It's also within this preference that you instruct iTunes to play videos in standard definition by default and show closed captions when they're available. But the most interesting settings here are Crossfade Songs, Sound Enhancer, and Sound Check:

- **Crossfade Songs.** This setting causes the end of each song to fade out and the beginning of the next track to fade in. For some people, this feature makes for a less jarring listening experience. You can set the length of the crossfade—1 to 12 seconds—with a slider. These settings don't transfer to the iPod.

- **Sound Enhancer.** This feature is a kind of audio filter that can expand and brighten the sound coming from iTunes tracks. It's worth playing with to see whether its results please you. These settings don't transfer to the iPod either.

- **Sound Check.** iTunes includes a Sound Check feature that you use to make the volumes of all your tracks similar. Without Sound Check, you may be listening to a Chopin prelude at a lovely, lilting volume and be scared out of your socks when the next track, AC/DC's "Highway to Hell," blasts through your brain. With Sound Check on, each track should be closer to the same relative volume. This preference is where you do that.

Sharing

iTunes allows you to easily share your music library or just specific playlists in it with other copies of iTunes running on a local network (and allows those iTunes libraries to be shared with you). You can share your library by enabling the Share My Library on My Local Network option.

To seek out other iTunes shared libraries, enable the Look for Shared Libraries option.

Store

As the name implies, this preference is where you tell iTunes how to interact with the iTunes Store. Options include Automatically Check for Available Downloads, Automatically Download Prepurchased Content, Automatically Download Missing Album Artwork, and Use Full Window for iTunes Store. All options but the last one are enabled by default.

Parental

Not all music and video is appropriate for all ages. Within the Parental preference, you can disable podcasts, radio, the iTunes Store (though optionally allow access to iTunes U), and shared libraries, as well as restrict content—certain movies, TV shows, and applications, and explicit material—from the iTunes Store.

Advanced

The Advanced preference is where you tell iTunes the location of your media files and how to organize them. In Chapter 9, I put this preference to good use in shifting an iTunes Library from a cramped startup drive to a more expansive external drive.

Working with the Info window

I talk about tagging a fair amount in this chapter. By *tagging*, I don't mean playing the kids' game, but practicing the subtle art of marking files with identifying bits of information (such as title, artist, album, and genre) so that you can locate and organize them more easily. You do all this in an item's Info window.

Tag, You're It

So how does iTunes know about tracks, artists, albums, and genres? Through something called ID3 tags. *ID3 tags* are just little bits of data included in a song file that tell programs like iTunes something about the file—not just the track's name and the album it came from, but also the composer, the album track number, the year it was recorded, and whether it's part of a compilation.

These ID3 tags are the key to creating great Smart Playlists. To view this information, select a track and choose File > Get Info. Click the Info tab in the resulting window, and you'll see fields for all kinds of things. You may find occasions when it's helpful to change the information in these fields. If you have two versions of the same song—perhaps one is a studio recording and another is a live recording—you could change the title of the latter to include *(Live)*.

A really useful field to edit is Comments. Here, you can enter anything you like and then use that entry to sort your music. If a particular track would be great to fall asleep to, for example, enter **sleepy** in the Comments field. Do likewise with similar tracks, and when you're ready to hit the hay, create a Smart Playlist that includes *Comment is sleepy*. With this technique under your belt, you can create playlists that fit particular moods or situations, such as a playlist that gets you pumped up during a workout.

Summary

Should a stranger stop you in the street and demand the format, bit rate, location of a particular track in your iTunes Library, this tab is where you'd look. Additionally, you'll discover the track's name, artist, album, sample rate, modification date, play count, and last-played date in the Summary pane.

Chapter 3: iPod touch As iPod   91

Info

This tab is where all the tagging business takes place. Here, you find fields for such information as name, artist, album, composer, comments, year, and track number, as well as a Genre menu (**Figure 3.10**). iTunes is pretty good about filling in this information for you, but at times, you may need to tag your own music—when iTunes doesn't recognize a ripped CD, for example, or when you've ripped someone else's mix CD and iTunes can't identify its tracks.

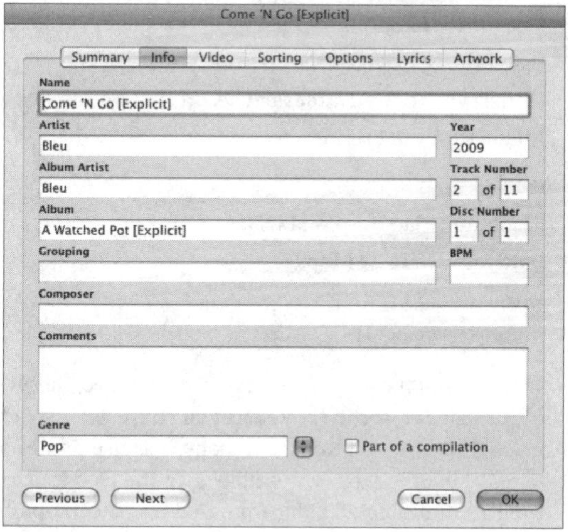

Figure 3.10

An Info window.

Video

When you import TV episodes from sources other than the iTunes Store, that video may lack the proper tags—show name, season, and episode number, for example. The Video tab contains fields for exactly that information.

Working with Supported Video Formats

Regrettably, you can't take just any video you pull from the Web or rip from a DVD and plunk it on your iPod. Your iPod has standards the video must meet before iTunes will allow it to touch the device.

Specifically, the videos must be in either MPEG-4 or H.264 format and must fit within these limits:

MPEG-4

Resolution: 640 by 480 pixels

Data rate: Up to 2.5 Mbps

Frame rate: 30 fps (frames per second)

Audio: Up to 48 kHz

H.264

Resolution: 640 by 480 pixels

Data rate: Up to 1.5 Mbps

Frame rate: 30 fps

Audio: Up to 48 kHz

What? If you have experience encoding video, these numbers will make sense to you; if they have you confused instead, don't fret. You needn't bone up on this technology, because iTunes provides a way to make your videos compatible with the iPod touch. Here's how: Drag an unprotected video (one that *isn't* a copy-protected TV show or video that you *haven't* purchased from the iTunes Store) onto the Library entry in iTunes' Source list.

If the video is compatible with iTunes, it will be added to the library; if not, the dragged icon will zip back to its original location. If the video isn't compatible, you can convert it with a utility such as Roxio Crunch, available for Windows and Macintosh for $40 (www.roxio.com), or the free, Intel-only Video Monkey (http://videomonkey.org).

Working with Supported Video Formats (continued)

Some videos that play in iTunes may be encoded at resolutions or data rates too high for the iPod to handle. Those files won't sync with your iPod, but you can make them compatible. To do that, select a video (listed in the Movies or TV Shows entry within iTunes' Source list), and choose Advanced > Create iPod or iPhone Version. This command creates an iPod- and iPhone-compatible version of the video, which you can sync to your iPod.

Note that converting a video for iPod compatibility doesn't replace the original, so it's not a bad idea to rename the converted version— *Casablanca (iPod),* for example—so that you can identify and sync the right one.

Sorting

Tracks can be sorted by their real name, artist, album artist, album, composer, and show—or by their sort name, sort artist, sort album artist, sort album, sort composer, and sort show. Why? Suppose that you really like Willie Nelson. As you probably know, Willie has performed duets with every living artist born between 1925 and 1994—sometimes on his albums and sometimes on the duet partner's album. If you want to listen to all-Willie-all-the-time, you might track down all those duet tracks that aren't on Willie's own albums and assign *Willie Nelson* as the sort artist for those tracks. Do that, and when you sort tracks by artist or search for *Willie Nelson*, you'll find these tracks bunched in with the tracks from Willie's albums.

Options

Within the Options pane, you can adjust a track's volume so that it's louder or softer, choose an equalizer (EQ) preset (see the sidebar "EQ and the iPod" toward the end of this chapter), select an item's media type, and choose a VoiceOver language (for speaking track titles when using an iPod nano or shuffle that supports VoiceOver). For videos, the media type will be music video, movie, TV show, podcast, or iTunes U; for audio files, it will be music, podcast, iTunes U, audiobook, or voice memo.

You can also impose start and stop times on a track. This feature is useful when you can't stand the first minute of a song or podcast and want to skip that minute automatically whenever you play the track. To do that, enable the Start Time option and then enter **1:00** in the text box.

You'll also see the Remember Playback Position, Skip When Shuffling, and Part of a Gapless Album options. The first two options are particularly useful for audiobook chapters that you may have ripped. You want to be able to pick up listening where you left off in a 30-minute chapter, and you don't want your iPod randomly playing the third chapter of *Harry Potter and the Usurious Audiobook Purchase* when you're working out.

The last option, Part of a Gapless Album, overrides any crossfade setting that you've applied to a song, preventing songs that should naturally flow together (think *Dark Side of the Moon* or concert recordings) from being crossfaded.

Finally, cock a keen eye at the Rating field in the middle of the pane. Here, you can rate your tracks with one to five stars. (You can also rate tracks by clicking the Rating column next to a track's name, as well as by selecting a track and choosing a rating from the Rating submenu of the File menu.) Rating your media now is helpful for creating Smart Playlists later, basing those playlists on songs and videos you enjoy.

Lyrics

You recall that your iPod can display lyrics, right? This pane is where you enter them. Regrettably, lyrics don't come with tracks that you purchase from the iTunes Store (no, not even with the premium-priced iTunes LPs that I discuss in Chapter 4). You're welcome to enter the lyrics by hand or search for them online. Music publishers have cracked down on Web sites that offer free lyrics, however, so these words are more difficult to find than they once were.

Artwork

iTunes is more than happy to seek out album artwork for you, but it locates artwork only for albums that are available from the iTunes Store. If you import an album that can't be had from the Store, a generic icon appears in Grid and Cover Flow views. You can add your own artwork simply by dragging a graphic file into the artwork field in the Artwork pane.

> **tip** You can tag multiple files simply by selecting more than one file and choosing File > Get Info. A Multiple Item Information window appears, and you can add tags therein for such things as artist, album, composer, comments, genre, artwork, and rating. This feature is handy for adding one piece of album artwork to a group of tracks.

Using the Music Application

Now that you've filled your iPod touch with tunes, you'd probably like to know how to find and play it. Follow along as I walk through the Music application of the iPod touch.

Cover Flow view

Tap the orange Music icon in the bottom-left corner of your iPod's Home screen, wait for the Playlists screen to appear (which it does by default when you first tap iPod), and immediately turn the iPod on its side. You're witnessing the iPod's Cover Flow view, which lets you browse your music collection by its album or program artwork (**Figure 3.11**). I don't care if you never choose to browse your music this way; Cover Flow is the music feature you'll choose first to impress your friends. They can't help but *oooh* in awe when you flick your finger across the screen and the artwork flips by.

Figure 3.11
*Cover Flow on
the iPod touch.*

Should you want to navigate your music in Cover Flow view, you can do so easily:

1. Turn the iPod touch to landscape orientation (it doesn't matter whether this turn places the Home button on the right or left side; the button works either way), and flick your finger across the display to move through your audio collection.

   Albums are sorted by the artist's first name, so *Al Green* appears near the beginning and *ZZ Top* appears close to the end.

2. When you find an album you want to listen to, tap its cover.

   The artwork flips around and reveals the track list of the album's contents (**Figure 3.12**).

Figure 3.12
The iPod's track list.

As with other lists on the iPod that may be longer than the screen, you're welcome to flick your finger up the display to move down through the list.

3. Tap the track you want to listen to.

   Playback begins from that track and plays to the end of the list in the order presented in the track list.

   To adjust volume in this view, use the Volume buttons on the side of the phone. To pause playback, tap the Play/Pause icon in the bottom-left corner of the screen or, if you're listening with the iPod's headset, press its Center button once.

4. To move to another album, tap the album-art thumbnail in the top-right corner of the cover, swipe your finger to the right or left, or tap the *i* icon in the bottom-right corner of the screen.

   Any of these actions will flip the track list back to the artwork.

note   While you're listening to the contents of one album, you're free to view the contents of another. Just flick your finger across the screen to move through your collection. Go ahead and tap an album to see its contents. It won't play until you tap a track.

Music Now Playing screen

Turn your iPod so that it's in portrait orientation, and Cover Flow disappears; it works only in landscape orientation. What you're left with when you flip the iPod to portrait orientation is the Music Now Playing screen. This screen is what you'll use to perform several tasks, including navigating through an album, fast-forwarding, switching on shuffle or repeat play, and rating your tracks. This screen differs from the Now Playing screen that you see when playing a video, podcast, or audiobook. (I discuss how it differs later in the chapter.)

This Now Playing screen has two main views: standard play and track list.

Standard play

The view you see first is straightforward. From the bottom of the screen to the top, you see a volume slider; play controls that include Previous/Rewind, Play/Pause, and Next/Fast Forward icons; album art; a Back icon; artist, track title, and album title information; and a Track List icon (**Figure 3.13**).

Figure 3.13
The Now Playing screen.

The volume slider operates like its real-world equivalent. Just drag the silver ball on the slider to the right to increase volume and to the left to turn the volume down. (You can use the iPod's mechanical volume buttons to adjust volume as well.)

The Previous/Rewind icon earns its double name because of its two jobs. Tap it once, and you're taken to the beginning of the currently play-ing track or chapter of the currently playing podcast or audiobook. Tap it twice, and you move to the previous track or chapter. Tap and hold, and the currently playing track rewinds.

The Play/Pause icon toggles between these two functions.

The Next/Fast Forward icon works like Previous/Rewind: Tap once to move to the next track in the track list or chapter in an audiobook or podcast; press and hold to fast-forward through the currently playing track.

I'll skip album art for a second and move to the Back icon in the top-left corner of the screen. Tap this icon, and you'll move to the currently selected track-view screen. If you've chosen to view your music by play-list, for example, you'll see your list of playlists. When you tap the Back icon and are taken to one of these screens, a Now Playing button appears in the top-right corner of the current screen. This icon appears whenever you're in the iPod area, making it easy to move to the Now Playing screen.

Track list

In the top-right corner of the Now Playing screen is the Track List icon. Tap this icon, and you get that album-cover flip effect again and a list of the current album's contents (**Figure 3.14** on the following page). (Naturally, if you have only a couple of tracks from that album on your iPod, you'll see just those tracks.) Just as you can in Cover Flow view, tap an entry in the track list to listen to that track. Again, tracks play in order from where you tapped.

Figure 3.14
*A track list in
the Now Playing
screen.*

The Track List screen also includes a means for rating tracks. Just above the track list, you'll see five gray dots. To assign a star rating from 1 to 5, simply tap one of the dots. Tap the fourth dot, for example, and the first four dots turn to stars. You can also wipe your finger across the dots to add or remove stars. These ratings are transferred to iTunes when you next sync your iPod touch. Tap the artwork image to flip the track list and return to the Now Playing screen.

Additional controls

While you're in the Now Playing screen, tap the artwork in the middle of the screen, and additional controls drop down from above (**Figure 3.15**). Starting from the left, you'll find a Repeat icon. Tap this icon once, and the contents of the currently playing album, audiobook, or podcast will repeat from beginning to end. Tap the Repeat icon twice, and just the currently playing selection will repeat.

Figure 3.15
*Tap the Now
Playing screen
to see additional
controls.*

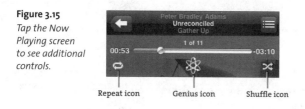

Repeat icon   Genius icon   Shuffle icon

A timeline with playhead comes next. To its left is the location of the
playhead in minutes and seconds—*1:40*, for example. To its right is the
track's remaining time. Drag the playhead with your finger to move to
a different position in the currently playing track. You can do this while
a track is playing and hear where you are as your drag (or *scrub*, as it's
known in the iTunes business).

More-Refined Scrubbing

If you used the iPod touch's scrubbing feature before the 3.0 software, you know how difficult it was to locate the exact spot you
wanted in a track; scrubbing wasn't a precision operation. That
changed with the iPod touch 3.0 software. Now you can scrub in
smaller increments than ever before.

To do that, tap and hold the playhead. When you do (and if your
thumb doesn't get in the way), you'll see the words *Hi-Speed
Scrubbing*. If you drag your finger to the left or right, you move
through the track in large increments. Ah, but drag your finger
down the screen, and those words change to *Half Speed Scrubbing*,
Quarter Speed Scrubbing, and *Fine Scrubbing*. Keep dragging until
you find an increment you're happy with and then drag your finger
to the left or right. The farther down the display your finger is, the
smaller increments the playhead will jump in.

To the far right is the Shuffle icon. Tap this icon once so that it turns blue and the contents of the current album are shuffled; tap it again to turn shuffle off.

If you've added lyrics to a track (as you can in the Lyrics tab of the track's Info window in iTunes), those lyrics will appear on the iPod's screen when you enter this view.

Below the timeline is the Genius icon. As you saw earlier in this chapter, Genius is a very cool feature—so cool, in fact, that it deserves to be called out. I do that in the next section.

True Genius

After you've enabled the Genius feature in iTunes and synced your iPod touch, you can create Genius playlists on your iPod. Here are two ways to do this.

1. Launch the Music app, and tap Playlists at the bottom of the screen.

2. Tap Genius Playlist at the top of the screen.

   The Songs screen appears.

3. Tap a song that you want to use as the basis of the Genius playlist.

   The iPod constructs a playlist of up to 25 tracks (including the one you selected) that it believes are related. The track you selected starts playing.

4. Tap the Back icon to view the playlist.

   Doing so takes you to the Genius screen, where you see the list of tracks (**Figure 3.16**). To create a new Genius playlist, tap New, and the process begins again. To have the iPod construct a different playlist based on the same selection, tap Refresh. Finally, if you want to save your playlist, tap Save.

Figure 3.16

The iPod's Genius Playlist screen.

When you tap Save, Genius creates a playlist that bears the name of the selected track. So, for example, if you based a Genius playlist on "Here Comes the Sun," the playlist will be called *Here Comes the Sun*. Its name is followed by a Genius icon in the list of playlists so that you know its origin.

Or . . .

1. While viewing the Now Playing screen, tap the screen so that the timeline appears near the top of the screen; then tap the Genius icon below the timeline (refer to Figure 3.15 earlier in this chapter).

    The iPod's progress icon appears briefly, followed by a Genius screen that features, at the top, the song you selected as the basis for the playlist. The up-to-24 additional songs appear below it.

2. Create a new Genius playlist, try again, or save the playlist.

When you sync your iPod touch to your Mac or PC, the Genius playlists you created on your iPod appear in your computer's copy of iTunes, marked with the Genius icon.

Podcasts and audiobooks

Start a podcast or audiobook playing on your iPod touch, and you'll notice that the controls at the bottom of the screen—Previous/Rewind, Play/Pause, and Next/Fast Forward—are exactly the same. The controls above are not.

Although you see the expected timeline and time readouts near the top of the screen, the icons you see just below them when playing an audio podcast, video podcast, or audiobook are different (**Figure 3.17**).

Figure 3.17
*Additional
controls for
listening to an
audio podcast.*

Email icon   30-Second   Speed icon
                    Rewind icon

Depending on which kind of media you're playing, all these icons shake out this way.

Email

This icon appears when you're playing a video or audio podcast. Tap this icon, and in most cases an unaddressed email message opens, bearing the message *Check out this podcast on iTunes,* followed by a link to that podcast. When the recipient clicks or taps that link, iTunes launches and takes her to that podcast's page.

I say *in most cases* because sometimes the email link does nothing—presumably because the iPod touch doesn't have the email address for the podcast and, therefore, can't embed it in an email message.

30-Second Rewind

Tap this icon while an audio podcast, video podcast, or audiobook plays; it jumps back 30 seconds and plays from that point.

Speed

With this icon, you can change the playback speed of an audio podcast or audiobook. By default, playback speed is set at 1x, which is normal speed. Tap the Speed icon once to change it to 2x, and the speed doubles (without changing pitch). Tap the icon again, and it changes to 1/2x, indicating that the audio plays at half speed (again, without changing pitch). One more tap takes you back to 1x.

Loop

The Loop icon appears in the far-left corner of the screen, below the timeline, when you listen to an audiobook. Tap the icon once, and the entire audiobook loops. Tap it twice, and the currently playing chapter loops.

Shuffle

The Shuffle icon appears in the far-right corner of the screen when you play a video podcast. If you activate it, when the currently playing video podcast concludes, the iPod shuffles to another episode of that same podcast. If you have only one episode of that podcast, you return to that podcast's screen rather than shuffle to an episode of a different video podcast.

Track List

In the top-right corner of the screen is the Track List icon—which in this case isn't really a track list. Instead, when you tap it, you see an audiobook's chapters or the chapters of an "enhanced" audio podcast. (What makes these podcasts "enhanced" is their inclusion of graphics and chapter markers.) To navigate easily through an audiobook or enhanced podcast, just tap the chapter you want to move to.

iPod Voice Control

If you have a 32 GB or 64 GB iPod touch released in late 2009, you can control audio playback to an extent. Just press and hold the Center button of the iPod's headset controller, and the iPod's Voice Control screen appears. Wait for the double beep, and issue any of the following commands to control music functions on the iPod:

- **"Play" or "Play music":** The iPod will play the last song that it believes you were listening to and then continues playing the album or playlist that the song is part of. If no last song was playing, the iPod picks a song at random.

- **"Pause":** The iPod pauses the currently playing track.

- **"Next song":** You get the next song in the album or playlist.

- **"Previous song":** You get the previous song in the album or playlist.

- **"Play *album*" (name of album):** If you say "Play album *Court and Spark*," and you have that album (or a portion of it) on your iPod touch, that's just what the iPod will do.

- **"Play *artist*" (name of artist):** Same idea here. Say "Play artist Jeff Lorber," and the iPod will pick a track by the estimable jazz keyboard player and then continue playing his work in random order.

- **"Play *playlist*" (name of playlist):** Shout out "Play playlist 50 Fabulous '70s Hits by '80s Artists!" to hear that playlist played from beginning to end.

- **"Shuffle":** Use this command to shuffle the currently playing playlist.

- **"What's playing?"** or **"What song is this?"** or **"Who sings this song?"** or **"Who is this song by?":** All these questions provide an answer along the lines of "Now playing *name of song* by *name of artist*."

- **"Genius"** or **"Play more like this"** or **"Play more songs like this":** Any command like these directs the Genius feature to play songs in the vein of the currently playing song.

- **"Cancel":** Never mind.

The Limits of Voice Control

Cool as Voice Control may be, it has limits. It won't respond, for example, to the following commands:

- **"Play 'Stairway to Heaven' "** (because it doesn't recognize individual track titles).

- **"Play the** *Macworld Podcast*" (because it can't be commanded to play podcasts unless those podcasts are part of a playlist).

- **"Shuffle off"** (because although you can turn shuffle on by voice, you can't turn it off the same way).

- **"Play** *Gone with the Wind*" (because Voice Control can't control videos).

- **"This song stinks!"** (which it may, but upon hearing this command, Voice Control won't assign a single-star rating to the currently playing track).

Music content views

The iPod's Music application provides several ways to organize your media. Look across the bottom of the screen (anywhere but in the Now Playing screen), and you'll see five icons for doing just that: Playlists; Artists; Songs; Albums; and More, which leads you to even more options (**Figure 3.18** on the following page).

Figure 3.18
*The icons you
find at the
bottom of most
Music-application
screens.*

note   If you've synced a Genius Mix to your iPod touch, those icons will be
Genius, Playlists, Artists, Songs, and More. The Album entry is now
located at the top of the More screen.

These icons are largely self-explanatory. If you've synced a Genius Mix to
your iPod touch, it (and others you've synced) are playable when you tap
Genius. To play one, just tap the Play icon on the screen. To navigate to
other Genius Mixes, swipe your finger from right to left.

When you tap Playlists, you'll see a list of all the playlists you've synced
to your iPod. Tap a playlist to move to a screen where all the tracks on the
playlist appear in the order in which they were arranged in iTunes. If you
tapped the Album heading when the playlist was displayed in iTunes, for
example, the tracks appear in that order. Tap a track, and you're taken to
the Now Playing screen, where the track begins playing.

Whenever you choose a list of tracks in one of these views, Shuffle is
the obvious entry at the top of the list. (I say *obvious* because if you
flick down, the Search field appears, thus becoming the first entry.)
Tap Shuffle, and the contents of that collection of tracks play in
random order.

Tap Artists, and you're presented with an alphabetical list of the artists
represented on your iPod. If your iPod has tracks from more than one
album by the selected artist, when you tap the artist's name, you'll be
taken to that artist's screen, which displays the titles of the artist's
represented albums (along with thumbnails of their cover art). To view

The On-The-Go Playlist

The iPod touch lets you create On-The-Go playlists—playlists you create on the fly—which you can create directly on the iPod touch rather than syncing them from iTunes. You can add individual songs or clumps of songs to this special playlist. The process works this way:

After tapping the Playlists icon, tap On-The-Go (the second entry after Genius Playlist), and a screen rises up from the bottom of the display, hinting that you've entered a special area of the Music application. Tap one of the entries at the bottom of the screen: Playlists, Artists, Songs, Albums, or More (and then one of the selections available in the More screen). If you tap Songs or Albums, an Add All Songs command appears at the top of the screen. Tap it, and that's exactly what happens. To add individual songs, tap them. When you tap an item, its name turns gray to indicate that it's been added to the On-The-Go playlist. Continue tapping icons at the bottom of the screen or in the More screen until you've added all the tracks you care to; then tap Done at the top of the screen.

When you return to the Playlists screen and tap On-The-Go, you'll see a list of all the tracks you've added through your endeavors. To edit the contents of this playlist, tap the Edit button at the top of the screen. In the Edit screen, you can tap the minus (–) icon next to a track to produce the Delete icon, which allows you to remove that track from the playlist (but not from your iPod), and the List icon, which you drag to change the position of the selected track in the playlist.

While you're in the Edit screen, you can tap the plus (+) icon to add more tracks to your On-The-Go playlist. Tap plus, and you're back to the view where you can add playlists, artists, songs, and so on.

To clear everything from the On-The-Go playlist, tap the On-The-Go playlist entry in the Playlists screen and then tap Clear in the resulting screen.

tracks from a particular album, tap its name. To view all songs by the artist, tap All Songs in this screen.

The Songs screen lists all the songs on your iPod. Like any list that contains several dozen (or more) entries, this one displays a tiny alphabet along the right side of the screen. To navigate to a letter quickly, tap it (as best you can, as the letters are really small) or slide your finger along the alphabet listing to dash through the list.

note If the first word of a list entry is *A* or *The*, the second word in the entry is used for sorting purposes. *The Beatles* is filed under *B*, for example, and *A Case of You* appears under *C*.

The Albums screen lists albums in alphabetical order and displays a thumbnail of the cover art next to the name of each album.

The iPod touch's display has limited space, yet you have many more ways to organize your media—by audiobooks, compilations, composers, and genres, for example. That's exactly what the More icon is for. Tap it, and you'll see just those items I list, as well as iTunes U and Podcasts entries. Tap these entries, and most of them behave pretty much as you'd expect, with a couple of variations:

- The Compilations entry lists only those albums that iTunes denotes as compilations. These items are usually greatest-hits collections, sound-tracks, or albums on which lots of artists appear—tribute albums or concert recordings, for example.

- The Podcasts screen displays all the podcasts on your iPod, along with their cover art. Tap a podcast title, and you're taken to a screen that lists all that podcast's episodes. Blue dots denote podcasts that you haven't listened to yet.

More Mucking

Unhappy that Apple chose to tuck the Albums entry in the More screen, yet left Artists easily accessible at all times? No worries. You can change what appears at the bottom of the Music application. Simply tap More and then the Edit icon in the top-left corner of the screen. Doing so produces a Configure screen that swipes up from the bottom of the display. Here, you'll see all the music category entries listed. Find one you like, and drag it over a icon on the bottom of the screen that you want to replace. The new entry takes the place of the old one, and the old entry is listed in the More screen. When you're done, tap Done.

Using the Videos Application

Like recent click-wheel iPods, the iPod touch plays videos. Some people would say that *unlike* these iPods, the touch makes videos actually watchable—bright and plenty big enough for personal viewing. Here are the ins and outs of iPod video.

Choosing and playing videos

Playing videos within the Video application is straightforward. Tap the Videos app at the bottom of the iPod's Home screen, and you'll see your videos listed by categories: Rented Movies (if any have been copied to the iPod), Movies, TV Shows, Music Videos, and Podcasts (**Figure 3.19** on the following page). Each video has a thumbnail image of its artwork next to it. Depending on the original source of the video, you may see title, artist, season, and episode information. The Rented Movies section, for example, tells you how many days you have left in the rental period to begin watching each movie (or how many hours you have left to finish watching a movie you've started). You'll definitely see the length of single videos—*1:56:26*, for example. If you have multiple episodes of a TV show, you'll see the name of the show as well as the number of episodes on the iPod.

Figure 3.19
An elongated view of the iPod's Videos screen.

To play a video, tap its list entry. Videos play only in landscape orientation, regardless of which way you have the iPod turned.

Navigating the video Now Playing screen

The video Now Playing screen is similar to the music Now Playing screen except that the play controls and timeline aren't visible unless you make them so. To display these controls, tap the video (**Figure 3.20**). You see the usual play controls—Previous/Rewind, Play/Pause, and Next/Fast Forward icons, and a volume slider—as well as a timeline near the top of the screen. The volume slider and timeline work just like they do in the music Now Playing screen. Drag the volume slider's volume indicator (represented by the silver dot) to increase or decrease volume, and move the timeline's playhead to a new location in the video.

Figure 3.20
*A video Now
Playing screen.*

Scale
icon

Chapters icon

> **tip** Cool as these controls look, you don't need to pull them up every time
> you want to adjust the volume. Just use the iPod's mechanical volume
> buttons. Or, if your iPod touch includes a headset controller, you can put its
> Volume Up and Volume Down buttons to good use.

You can advance to the next chapter in a video by tapping the Next/Fast
Forward icon. (If the video has no chapters, nothing happens when you
tap this icon.) If a movie has chapters, you can also tap the Chapters icon
that appears to the right of the Next/Fast Forward icon and choose the
chapter you want from the Chapter Guide menu that appears. This icon
won't appear when you view a movie without chapters.

If you tap and hold Next/Fast Forward, the video speeds up. To retreat a
chapter, tap Previous/Rewind twice (tap once to return to the beginning
of the currently playing chapter). The play controls list the chapter you're
currently watching—*Chapter 13 of 32,* for example.

The video Now Playing screen has a control you may not have seen
before: the Scale icon, in the top-right corner of the screen. Tapping this
icon toggles the display between Fill Screen and Fit to Screen. (You can
also toggle these views by double-tapping the display.)

Fill Screen is similar to DVDs you've seen that say the movie was altered to fit your TV. The iPod's entire screen is taken up by video, but some of the content may be chopped off in the process.

Fit to Screen displays the entire video, similar to a letterbox movie you may have seen. In this view, you may have black bars at the top and bottom or on the sides.

When you finish watching a video, tap the screen and then tap the Done icon in the top-left corner of the screen. You'll return to the Videos screen.

tip **By default, the iPod remembers where you left off. When you next play this video, it will take up from the point where you stopped playback. To change this behavior so that you always start from the beginning of a video, tap the Video entry in the Settings screen and then tap the Start Playing entry. You can choose From Beginning or Where Left Off.**

Applying Music Settings

Like other iPod touch applications, the Music and Videos apps get their own little entries in the iPod's Settings screen. I'll start with Music Settings.

Shake to Shuffle

If you'd like to engage the iPod's shuffle feature, just switch on this option and give the iPod a vigorous shake. This shake does more than shuffle; it also immediately causes the iPod to stop playing the current song and move to another one. So even though you can't vent your frustration at a particularly awful song via Voice Control, you're free to violently shake the iPod while shouting "*I . . . hate . . . this . . . song!*"

Sound Check

I talk about Sound Check in iTunes earlier in this chapter. This feature, when enabled in iTunes, also works on the iPod. You switch it on within the Music Settings screen.

EQ

EQ (or *equalization*) is the process of boosting or cutting certain frequencies in the audio spectrum—making the low frequencies louder and the high frequencies quieter, for example. If you've ever adjusted the bass and treble controls on your home or car stereo, you get the idea.

The iPod comes with the same EQ settings as iTunes:

- Off
- Acoustic
- Bass Booster
- Bass Reducer
- Classical
- Dance
- Deep
- Electronic

- Flat
- Hip Hop
- Jazz
- Latin
- Loudness
- Lounge
- Piano
- Pop

- R & B
- Rock
- Small Speakers
- Spoken Word
- Treble Booster
- Treble Reducer
- Vocal Booster

Although you can listen to each EQ setting to get an idea of what it does, you may find it easier to open iTunes; choose Window > Equalizer; and then, in the resulting Equalizer window, choose the various EQ settings from the window's pop-up menu. The equalizer's ten band sliders will show you which frequencies have been boosted and which have been cut. Any slider that appears above the 0 dB line indicates a frequency that has been boosted. Conversely, sliders that appear below 0 dB indicate frequencies that have been cut.

EQ and the iPod

Having EQ built into iTunes and the iPod is great, but the interaction between iTunes and the iPod in regard to EQ is a little confusing. Allow me to end that confusion.

In iTunes, you can assign an EQ setting to a song individually by clicking the song, pressing Command-I (Mac) or Ctrl+I (Windows), clicking the Options tab, and then choosing an EQ setting from the Equalizer Preset menu. When you move songs to your iPod, these EQ settings move right along with them, but you won't be able to use them unless you configure the iPod correctly.

If, for example, you have EQ switched off on the iPod, songs that have assigned EQ presets won't play with those settings. Instead, your songs will play without the benefit of EQ. If you set the iPod's EQ to Flat, the EQ setting that you preset in iTunes will play on the iPod. If you select one of the other EQ settings on the iPod (Latin or Electronic, for example), songs without EQ presets assigned in iTunes will use the iPod EQ setting. Songs with EQ settings assigned in iTunes will use the iTunes setting.

If you'd like to hear how a particular song sounds on your iPod with a different EQ setting, start playing the song on the iPod, choose Settings > Music > EQ, and then select one of the EQ settings. The song will immediately take on the EQ setting you've chosen, but this setting won't stick on subsequent playback. If you want to change the song's EQ more permanently, you must do so in iTunes.

Volume Limit

Though Apple takes pains to warn you in the iPod's documentation that blasting music into your ears at full volume can lead to hearing loss, some people just can't get enough volume. If your child is one of those people, consider setting a volume limit for the iPod's headphone port. To do so, tap Volume Limit in the Music Settings screen, and in the resulting Volume Limit screen, use the volume slider to set an acceptable volume. (Have a track playing when you do this so that you can listen to the effect.) To keep your kid from changing your settings, tap Lock Volume Limit. You'll see a Set Code screen, where you'll enter and confirm a four-digit security code (**Figure 3.21**). When this code is set, the Lock Volume Limit icon changes to Unlock Volume Limit. Tap this button, and you'll be prompted for the security code.

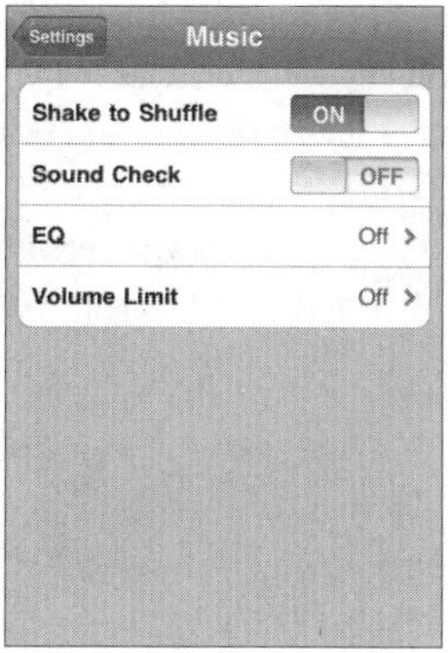

Figure 3.21

Setting a volume limit for the iPod touch.

Applying Video Settings

And now to the settings that you find when you tap Video in the Settings screen.

Start Playing

I mention this setting in a little tip earlier in the chapter. Start Playing lets you choose whether videos that you return to later play from where they left off or from the beginning.

Closed Captioning

Some videos that you purchase from the iTunes Store include closed captions. You can choose to show those captions by flicking this switch to On.

Widescreen

This first option in the TV Out section of the Video Settings screen lets you specify whether videos played on the iPod connected to a television set with a compatible cable or Dock will play in widescreen or standard-screen view. Why wouldn't you choose widescreen if your iPod contains a widescreen movie? If you have such a movie and are attempting to display it on a small-screen TV set, the picture could be pretty narrow and tiny. If you turn this option off, the entire TV screen will be filled with the picture (though both sides of the movie will be clipped off so that this screen-filling can take place).

TV Signal

The world has two major TV standards: NTSC (used in North and South America and much of Asia) and PAL (used in much of Europe and Australia). The iPod touch can output video to a television set in either standard. You use this setting to choose NTSC or PAL.

4

The iPod's Stores

You know that constant use gives you the power to drain your iPod touch's battery. In what some people might view as a turnabout-is-fair-play situation, your iPod has the power to drain your wallet. Its means for doing so are two Apple-owned online emporiums accessible from your iPod touch: the iTunes Store and the App Store. The former lets you browse, purchase, and download music, videos, podcasts, and iTunes U content over a Wi-Fi connection with nothing more than your iPod and an iTunes account linked to your credit card. The App Store is where you find free and commercial add-on applications (made by Apple as well as third parties) that you can also download over Wi-Fi.

In this chapter, I examine the workings of each store.

Prepare to Shop

Ready to shop? Great. You'll first need to sign up for an iTunes account, and I've found that easiest to do from within the iTunes application on your computer. Here's how.

What you need

Naturally, you need a Mac or a Windows PC and a copy of iTunes. It's not necessary to have an iPod to take advantage of The Store. Media purchased at The Store can be played on your computer; music can be burned to CD; and because Apple now sells music free of copy protection, the music you purchase there can be played on any device that supports the AAC format (discussed in Chapter 3).

Also, although you can access The Store via any Internet connection, you'll find it far more fun to shop with a reasonably speedy broadband connection. A 4-minute song weighs in at around 8 MB. Such a download takes next to no time over a DSL, cable, or fiber-optic connection but can be terribly slow over a poky Wi-Fi connection or—heaven forbid!—a slothlike dial-up modem. Even with a moderately fast broadband connection, you could wait up to an hour to download a full-length movie from The Store.

As these pages go to print, The Store is available in 77 countries. Which store you're allowed to purchase media from depends on the issuing country of your credit card. If you have a credit card issued in Germany, for example, you can purchase media only from the German iTunes Store (though you don't physically have to be in Germany to do this; again, the credit card determines where you can shop).

Sign on

You're welcome to browse The Store the first time you fire up iTunes, but to purchase media, you must establish an account and sign in. Fortunately, Apple makes the process pretty easy.

With your computer connected to the Internet, launch iTunes, and click the iTunes Store entry in iTunes' Source list; then click the Sign In button in the top-right corner of the iTunes window. If you have either an Apple ID and password or an AOL screen name and password, enter them and click the Sign In button; otherwise, click the Create New Account button.

When creating an account, you'll be required to agree to the iTunes Store's terms-of-service agreement, enter a valid email address, and create a password. Along the way, you'll enter some personal information so that Apple can identify you, if need be.

Finally, you'll be asked for a credit card number and your name, address, and phone number. Click Done and . . . you're done. You're now a member in good standing.

Obtaining an Apple ID via the iPod touch

Again, I've found it easier to get an iTunes account from my computer, but you can also get one directly from your iPod touch when it's connected to a Wi-Fi network. Just follow these steps:

1. Tap Settings in the Home screen.

2. Tap Store.

3. In the resulting Store screen, tap Create New Account.

4. In the resulting New Account screen, confirm the country or region that matches your credit card's billing address, and tap Next.

5. At the bottom of the Terms of Service screen that appears, tap Agree; then tap Agree again when you're asked to confirm your agreement.

(continued on next page)

Obtaining an Apple ID
via the iPod touch (continued)

6. Fill out the requested information in the New Account screen:

   - Your email address

   - A password (enter it twice for verification purposes)

   - A question that only you are likely to know the answer to, such as the name of your first pet, and the answer to that question

   - The month and day of your birth

7. Still in the New Account screen, choose whether to subscribe to Apple's marketing email messages; then tap Next.

8. In the resulting screen, provide your credit card and billing information.

   It's time to pay up—or to prove that you *can* pay up—by entering your credit card type (Visa, MasterCard, Amex, or Discover), its number and security code, its expiration month and year, and your billing address.

9. Tap Next.

   Your encrypted information is sent to Apple. If you pass muster, you're ready to go.

The iPod's iTunes Store

At one time, the iPod touch's version of the iTunes Store was called the iTunes Wi-Fi Music Store, so named because you could shop only for music (to obtain videos or podcasts, you had to use iTunes on your computer), and you could do so only over a Wi-Fi connection. iPod touch owners are still confined to Wi-Fi, as the iPod doesn't support any other wireless networking protocol. (iPhone owners can download content via EDGE and 3G networks.)

Today's iTunes Store is far more capable. Now you can download almost any content offered by the iTunes Store directly to the iPod; the sole exception is HD movies (see the following note).

note **Although you can't download HD movies to your iPod touch, you can purchase them on your iPod. When you do, an iPod-compatible standard-definition version of the movie is downloaded to your iPod touch (if you're on a Wi-Fi network), and the HD version is made available to you within the copy of iTunes on your computer.**

Although this store's face is far less crowded than that of the full-size iTunes Store, the selection is no different. You can choose among the same millions of tracks, podcasts, TV shows, music videos, movies, and iTunes U content in this pocket-size version of The Store *and* in the iTunes Store available via iTunes. The feature works this way.

Browsing the little store

Tap the iTunes icon on the iPod touch's Home screen while you're connected to a Wi-Fi network, and the iTunes Store screen appears. Across the bottom of the screen, you see Music, Videos, Podcasts, Search, and More icons. Tap More, and you see Audiobooks, iTunes U, and Downloads. Here's what to expect.

Music

Tap Music, and you're taken to The Store's music section. Across the top of the screen are three buttons: New Releases, Top Tens, and Genres. These buttons work much as they do in the same-named areas of the full-grown iTunes Store's home page (which I hope you'll take the time to explore).

New Releases. Here, you see a list of the week's coolest additions—singles as well as albums. To preview or purchase one of these items, tap it to move to that item's screen. (I discuss the workings of this screen shortly.) In addition to the week's new releases, you're likely to see buttons for accessing free tracks and music videos and for viewing the hottest items currently available. At the very bottom of the screen is an Account button that displays your iTunes account email address—*example6@mac.com*, for example—along with the amount of any credit you have (*$25 Credit,* for example, if you've redeemed an iTunes gift card). Tap that, and you're offered the option to view your account details, sign out, or forget the whole thing by tapping Cancel.

At the bottom of the list of new releases, you'll see a Redeem item. As its name hints, you tap this item to access the Redeem screen, where you enter the code for an iTunes gift card or gift certificate. Just tap in the Code field, and the iPod's keyboard appears. After you enter the code, tap the Redeem button in the top-right corner of the screen to send the code to Apple.

Top Tens. This section features top songs and albums organized within particular genres. Tap Alternative, for example, and the next screen includes two large buttons: Top Songs and Top Albums (**Figure 4.1**). Tap one to see the top ten items of that kind. To see the complete list of Top Ten genres, tap the More Top Tens button near the bottom of the screen.

Genres. This section lists popular genres (Pop, Alternative, Hip-Hop/Rap, Rock, and Country, as I write this chapter). To view the complete list of genres, tap the More Genres button near the bottom of the screen. What you see when you tap a genre depends on the genre. When I tap Rock, for example, I see new releases. When I tap Soundtrack, I see titles offered below an In Theaters heading. Tapping Classical, Singer/Songwriter, or Jazz displays a list of albums. The top of each screen includes a couple of buttons that you can tap to go to albums that The Store believes worthy of your attention.

Figure 4.1
A Top Tens screen.

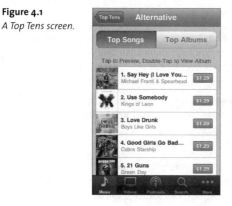

What's the Cost?

At one time, you knew exactly what you'd pay when you visited the iTunes Store: 99 cents for a single music track and $9.99 for an album. With all the media now available in The Store and Apple's adoption of variable pricing for much of it, that situation has changed. Here's the rundown:

- **Music.** Singles are priced at 69 cents, 99 cents, or $1.29. The most popular current tracks are $1.29. Albums cost $9.99 on average, but you can find bargains in the $7 and $8 range, as well as albums that cost $2 and $3 more. iTunes LPs (albums that contain enhanced material) are usually priced a few dollars more than the unenhanced versions. Albums that ship on two or more physical CDs cost quite a bit more, naturally.

(continued on next page)

What's the Cost? (continued)

- **Music videos.** Each video costs $1.99.

- **TV shows.** In most cases, standard-definition TV episodes are $1.99 each. (Such HBO shows as *The Sopranos* and *Rome* cost $2.99 per standard-definition episode.) High-definition TV episodes cost $2.99.

  TV seasons are priced according to the number of episodes they contain and the format they're in: HD or standard definition. You sometimes get a break for buying a season, but more often than not, you pay the aggregate price of all the episodes.

- **Purchased movies.** Apple characterizes movies as being library (meaning *older*) or new. Standard-definition library titles are $9.99; new standard-definition titles are $14.99. As I write this chapter, all HD titles are $20. Similar to iTunes LPs, iTunes Extras movies contain bonus material. These movies cost $15.

- **Rental movies.** Standard-definition library titles are $2.99, and new library titles in standard definition are $3.99. Library HD rentals are $3.99, and new HD rentals are $4.99. After you download a rental movie, you have 30 days to watch it. After you start watching it, you have 24 hours to finish it; the movie is automatically removed from the iPod after that period. During those 24 hours, you can watch the movie as many times as you like.

- **Audiobooks.** The pricing of audiobooks is all over the map. You can find some for just over $10, whereas others can cost up to $50 (because, apparently, the real magic of the Harry Potter novels is that they can command these kinds of prices).

- **Podcasts and iTunes U.** Free.

- **Applications.** This is completely up to the developer, but you'll find a lot of applications that are absolutely free or only a dollar.

Videos

The Videos area of The Store is where you can rent or purchase movies, purchase TV shows or entire TV seasons, and buy music videos. Tap the Videos button at the bottom of the screen, and you see a layout similar to the Music screen, with three buttons across the top: Movies, TV Shows, and Music Videos.

Movies. The Movies screen displays a couple of featured movies at the top (hot new releases, as I write this chapter). Below is a New Releases area with 30 entries; below that are Top Tens and Genres entries. Each entry lists the movie's genre (such as Comedy or Drama), its title, its user rating (1 to 5 stars, including half-stars), and the number of ratings it has received (*128 Ratings*, for example).

Tap a movie, and you see that movie's screen, where you can buy or rent it (if rental is an option—not all movies are for rent), as well as watch a preview of the movie. To do one of these things, tap the appropriate button. Below the buttons is a Reviews button that displays a five-star scale, reflecting the average rating given by people who chose to submit reviews. These people may or may not have purchased or rented that movie from iTunes (and may not have seen it at all, so take some reviews with a grain of salt). Tap that button, and you'll see the average rating and the number of people who have rated the movie. Below are user reviews, complete with title, text, date, and rating.

If you'd like to write a review of your own, tap the Write a Review button at the top of the screen. You'll be prompted for your iTunes password. Enter it, and you go to the Submit Review screen, where you can enter a rating, title, and review. To submit the review, just tap Send.

TV Shows. This section works almost exactly the same way as the Movies area. The main difference is that the items in this window are entire series (*The Wire*, for example) rather than single episodes. Tap a show, and you're taken to the season screen, where you can purchase individual episodes and, sometimes, entire seasons. These screens carry no Preview button. Instead, just tap an episode title, and the movie-player window displays a preview. TV Shows screens also have a Reviews button.

Music Videos. Same idea here. You see a couple of featured items at the top of the screen, a list of music videos below, and Top Tens and Genres menus. Tap a video, and you see the Buy and Preview buttons, along with the tapworthy reviews entry. In most cases, you also find a More by This Artist button. Tap it to see a screen listing other music videos by that artist.

Podcasts

We've been through all this before, right? The Podcasts screen has its own three buttons: What's Hot, Top Tens, and Categories. If you read the section on the Music and Videos areas, you have a solid idea of how The Store works. These buttons show you exactly what they say they do: popular podcasts of the day, the top ten podcasts in specific categories (News & Politics, Sports & Recreation, Technology, Comedy, Music, and More Top Tens, at this writing), and featured podcasts in the same categories I just listed. Podcasts come in both audio and video form, and all of them are free.

Search

Search is very iPod touch-like. Tap this button, and a Search field appears. Tap this field, and the iPod's keyboard appears. Type a song title, album title, or artist name in the Search field; as you type, suggestions appear below. When the result you desire appears, tap it.

The resulting screen displays a variety of media—including some that you may not expect. I searched for *Led Zeppelin*, and the results screen included "Stairway to Heaven" (of course), the *Mothership* album, two popular songs ("Kashmir" and "Black Dog"), two albums, three TV episodes (the TV show *NewsRadio* used "Led Zeppelin" in the title of three of its episodes), two movies, a couple of podcasts, two TV seasons (*NewsRadio* again), and two audiobooks. As you can see, a search can pull up a lot of unexpected results.

More

When you tap the More button at the bottom of the screen, you see three entries: Audiobooks, iTunes U, and Downloads. I needn't walk you through the first two. Just understand that The Store, like Audible.com, sells audiobooks that you can play on an iPod, iPhone, or your computer. Like music tracks, audiobooks can be burned to CD. You already know that iTunes U is the educational area of The Store, where you can download lectures, classes, and concerts offered, for the most part, by universities and colleges. Again, iTunes U content is free.

Downloads. As you might expect, this area is where you can watch the progress of the content you're downloading. It works like this: When you tap a price, it turns into a Buy Now button. Tap that button, and the item swoops down onto the Downloads icon, at which point you're prompted for your iTunes password (the same password that you use at the iTunes Store).

An icon on the Downloads button blinks, indicating the number of items that the iPod is downloading. Tap this icon, and a screen shows you the progress of the download (**Figure 4.2** on the following page). After the item has downloaded, you can play it on the iPod. When you next sync your iPod, the tracks you've purchased will be transferred from the iPod to your computer.

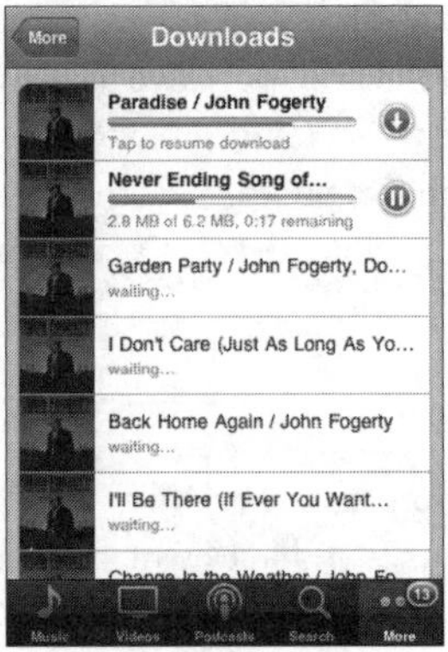

Figure 4.2
The Downloads screen lets you watch the progress of music coming to your iPod.

When these tracks are downloaded for the first time, a new playlist appears below the Store heading in the computer-based version of iTunes' Source list. That playlist is called Purchased on *nameofiPod*, where *nameofiPod* is the name of your iPod. After these tracks are in your iTunes Library, they behave like any others you own. You can burn music tracks to disc, and you can play any media on any of your authorized computers or any iPods and iPhones you own.

note If an album you purchase on the iPod is bundled with extra content (such as a digital booklet and/or videos), when you sync the iPod with your computer to download the music to it and connect to the iTunes Store, the extra content will download to iTunes automatically.

The Downloads screen also offers a shortcut to just those music tracks you've purchased on your iPod since you last synced the iPod. Tap the Purchased arrow in the top-right corner of the Downloads screen, and the iPod application opens and displays the Purchased on iPod playlist, which contains those purchased tracks.

Browsing at Starbucks

Walk into a Starbucks outlet and tap the iTunes application, and your iPod is likely to display a Starbucks button. When you tap that button, your iPod will tell you the name of the track that's currently playing in that store, as well as recently played tracks. Using the Starbucks interface, you can purchase any of these tracks.

The App Store

The App Store is a service, hosted by Apple, that lets you download applications created by Apple and third-party developers to your iPod touch, iPhone, or (via the iTunes Store) computer.

The App Store offers applications that you must pay for as well as scads of free ones, so even the most cheapskate iPod touch owners among us will find lots to like at this store. In this section, I show you how it works.

Browsing the App Store

The App Store offers an interface similar to what you find at the iTunes Store. Tap the App Store icon on the iPod's Home screen, and along the bottom of the resulting App Store screen, you'll see the five icons necessary to make your shopping experience as enjoyable as possible. The icons break down this way.

Featured

Tap the first icon in the row, and you move to the Featured screen. You'll find three buttons at the top: New, What's Hot, and Genius.

New. Tap New, and you'll see a list of notable applications—some free, some for sale—that have been added to the App Store recently

(**Figure 4.3**). Each entry includes the application's name, its maker, its user review rating (one to five stars), the number of reviews it's received, and its price. At the bottom of this list, you'll find the now-familiar Redeem entry, which works exactly as it does in the iTunes Store app.

Figure 4.3
Featured apps from the App Store.

What's Hot. When you tap What's Hot at the top of this screen, you see a list of the most-downloaded applications on the service. Each application bears the same information: name, maker, rating, number of reviews, and price.

Genius. This button, which is new with iPod touch software 3.0, operates very much like Apple's Genius playlists. You volunteer to participate by switching Genius on for apps. You do this by tapping Genius, tapping the Turn On Genius button in the resulting screen, entering your Apple ID password, and agreeing to the terms of service by tapping Agree at the bottom of the agreement. Then you see a list of 15 applications, recommended to you based on the other applications that you currently have on your iPod touch. To see another 15 recommendations, tap the More Recommendations button at the bottom of the list.

note That's correct—Genius makes its recommendations only on the apps that you have on your iPod. You could have hundreds more in iTunes, but those apps may as well not exist as far as the App Genius is concerned.

As I write this chapter, the top of the New and What's Hot screens show two applications or categories (Hot New Games, for example) in a banner. In Apple's estimation, these applications (or classes of applications) are too cool or too popular to miss.

Categories

If you'd like to browse the App Store for particular kinds of applications—games, finance, or productivity, for example—tap the Categories icon that appears in the second position at the bottom of the screen. The Categories screen is where you'll find applications listed in categories, including (at this writing) Games, Entertainment, Utilities, Social Networking, Music, Productivity, Lifestyle, Reference, Travel, Sports, Navigation, Healthcare & Fitness, News, Photography, Finance, Business, Education, Weather, Books, and Medical. Tap any of these categories except Games, and the resulting category screen includes three buttons that make it easier to find the apps you want: Top Paid, Top Free, and Release Date. When you tap Games, you're offered a screen that includes game genres, much like the one in iTunes. Tap a genre of game—Arcade, for example—and you'll see the Top Paid, Top Free, and Release Date buttons, along with a list of 25 games below.

Top 25

Featuring Top Paid, Top Free, and Top Grossing buttons at the top of the screen, Top 25 is what it says—a list of the 25 most-downloaded or most-money-generating applications at the App Store (**Figure 4.4** on the following page). Scroll to the bottom of any of these lists to find a Show Top 50 entry. Tap it, and another 25 entries appear, slightly less "top" than the first 25.

Figure 4.4
A Top 25 screen.

Search

Search is for those times when you think, "Hmm . . . Priscilla said something about a cool new app, but the only part of its name I remember
is *monkey*." Just tap Search, tap in the Search field, and type **monkey** on
the iPod's keyboard. You'll be sure to find the application you're after in
the list that appears. Tap the application's name, and you'll see its listing
along with the usual information—name, company, yada, as well as yada.

> **tip** Search produces results not only for product names, but company
> names too. If you know the company but not the name of the applica-
> tion, no worries—just search for the company name and tap it. Any applications
> offered by that company appear in the list of results.

Updates

Just like the applications you have on your computer, iPod touch applications are updated by their developers to fix problems and offer new
features. When an application you've downloaded has been updated—
and Apple has made that update available—the Update icon at the
bottom of the App Store screen bears a red circle with a number inside
it, indicating how many updates are available. The App Store icon on the
Home screen also adopts this icon.

When updates are available, you can choose to update single applications or click the Update All button in the top-right corner of the screen. Your iPod moves to the Home screen, and the updated versions of the applications begin to download. The progress of the download is shown in the form of a blue progress bar at the bottom of the application's icon.

Updating Applications in iTunes

You can also update your applications within iTunes. Select Applications in iTunes' Source list, and any applications you've downloaded from within iTunes (or downloaded on your iPod touch or iPhone and then synced back to iTunes) appear as a series of icons. Click one of these icons, choose File > Get Info, and click the Summary tab in the resulting window, and you'll see how large the application is, its version, who purchased it (and with which account), and the purchase date.

In the bottom-right section of the Applications window are two links: Check for Updates and Get More Applications. Click the first link, and a dialog box appears that reads *Updates for some of the applications in your iTunes Library are available. Would you like to view the available updates now?* Click the View Updates button, and you're taken to iTunes' My App Updates page, where updates for the applications you own appear. You can download individual updates by clicking the Get Update button next to the application or simply click the Download All Free Updates button in the top-right corner of the window to download all updates.

After you enter your iTunes password, the updates start downloading. You can check the progress of the downloads by clicking the Downloads entry in the Store area of iTunes' Source list. When the updates are downloaded, just sync your iPod to iTunes, and the updated versions of the applications will be copied to your iPod.

Managing applications

Now that you've found the applications you're after, you'll want to learn more about them and then start downloading the ones you want.

Navigating the Info screen

An application's Info screen is both the gateway to downloading the thing and a source of information about it (**Figure 4.5**). Here, you'll find the name of the application, the name of the developer, a star rating based on user reviews, the number of reviews, a price button that you tap to purchase the app, a link to those reviews, a description and screen shots of the application, developer contact information, post date, version, size, and rating.

A Tell a Friend button also appears in this screen. Tap it, and a new unaddressed email message opens, containing the name of the application in the Subject field and the words *Check out this application:* followed by a link to the application in the message body. The recipient of this message need only click the link; as long as he has a current copy of iTunes installed on his computer, iTunes will launch and take him to the iTunes Store page that's devoted to this

Figure 4.5
Elongated view of an app's Info screen.

application. (I discuss the iTunes Store's relationship with iPod touch and iPhone applications shortly.)

Reviews work similarly to the reviews for music in the iTunes app. The difference is that you're not allowed to review an app unless you've actually downloaded it. This helps prevent useless "This costs too much!" or "I hate cheese!" reviews that can drag down an app's rating.

Finally, there's the Report a Problem button. Tap it, and a Report a Problem screen appears, offering three choices: The Application Has a Bug, This Application Is Offensive, and My Concern Is Not Listed Here. These choices are followed by a Comments field where you can express yourself more thoroughly. Tap Report to send your report to Apple.

Downloading applications

Tap the entry for the application you want to download. Tap its price (yes, even if it's marked Free) and then tap Install. You'll be prompted for, at the very least, your iTunes password. (I say *at least* because if you were signed in to the iTunes Store the last time you synced your iPod, you won't be prompted for your iTunes account when you attempt to download something from the App Store. If you're using the App Store for the first time and aren't signed in to your iTunes account within iTunes, you'll be prompted for both your account address and password.)

Enter your password with the iPod's keyboard, and tap OK. The iPod moves to the Home screen, shows a dimmed icon for the application you're downloading, and displays Loading and then Installing progress bars at the bottom of the screen. When the application is fully loaded, the Installing progress bar disappears, and the icon takes on its full color and brightness. To launch the application, do as you do with any application on the iPod: Tap its icon.

The next time you sync your iPod with iTunes, any applications you've added to it—or that have been updated on the iPod—will be copied to iTunes' Applications area.

5

Mail, Contacts, and Calendar

Can't figure out how to copy your notes and screen shots from your iPod to a computer that's not synced with your iPod or how to receive documents that you can view on your iPod? Or is your life so tied to email that you can't stand to be away from your computer for more than a couple of hours? If so, you and the iPod's Mail application are about to become best friends.

Speaking of friends, little good it is to have the desire to email your friends from your iPod only to discover that you can't recall their addresses. Fortunately, you needn't possess an infallible memory for this kind of information when you can store it all in the Contacts application.

It's unlikely that you'll keep those friends if you routinely stand them up because you've forgotten the time and place to meet them. This needn't happen either. The iPod includes a Calendar application that lets you sync your schedule with your Mac or Windows PC, as well as create calendar events on the go. In this chapter, I explain the ins and outs of all three applications.

Using Mail

Mail is a real email client, much like the one you use on your computer. With it, you can send and receive email messages, as well as send and receive a limited variety of email attachments. You can receive and play such audio attachments as MP3, AAC, WAV, and AIFF. You can view received JPEG graphics files, text, and HTML; Microsoft Word, Excel, and PowerPoint documents; iWork Pages, Keynote, and Numbers files; and Adobe PDF documents. Regrettably, you can't edit any of the files you receive; they're read-only.

Mail is limited in some other ways:

- Unlike all modern computer-based email clients, the iPod touch has no spam filter and no feature for managing mailing lists.

- You can't flag messages or apply rules that allow Mail to sort or copy certain messages (those from a particular sender, for example) into specific mailboxes.

- Speaking of mailboxes, you can't create new mailboxes on the iPod, either. Instead, you must create them on your computer or on the Web, and you can do so only with IMAP accounts; they'll appear in Mail after you sync the mail accounts on your computer with the iPod.

The iPod is capable of sending and receiving email over a Wi-Fi connection only. Unlike the iPhone, the iPod touch doesn't support the EDGE and 3G wireless networking protocols offered by mobile phone carriers.

Now that you know what Mail can and can't do, you're ready to look at how to use it.

Creating an account

When you first synced your iPod to your computer, you were asked whether you wanted to synchronize your email accounts to the device. If you chose to do so, your iPod is nearly ready to send and receive messages. All you may have to do now is enter a password for your email account in the Mail, Contacts, Calendars setting.

But I'm getting ahead of myself. Rather than start in the middle, with a nearly configured account, I'll start at the beginning so that you can follow the iPod's account-setup procedure from start to finish. In the next few pages, I examine how to configure Exchange, Web-based (MobileMe, Gmail, Yahoo, and AOL), and IMAP and POP accounts.

Configuring an Exchange account

Let me take care of corporate readers first by outlining the steps necessary to create an Exchange account:

1. Tap the Settings icon in the iPod's Home screen and then tap Mail, Contacts, Calendars.

2. Tap Add Account, and in the resulting screen, tap Microsoft Exchange.

3. In the Exchange screen that appears, enter your email address, user name, password, and a description along the lines of *Company Email*.

   Your IT department or manager should be able to provide this info.

4. Tap Next.

   The iPod attempts to connect to the Exchange server.

If the connection is successful, you're pretty well set. If it isn't, another Exchange screen will ask for the same information you provided before, as well as the server address. Again, the Exchange server administrator should be able to give you this information. The address in question here is the address of the front-end server—the one that greets your iPod when it attempts to connect to the company server.

When this information is configured properly, the iPod attempts to log on to the server via a Secure Sockets Layer (SSL) connection. If it can't do so, it tries a nonsecure connection.

If SSL isn't configured correctly, you can change those settings by tapping the name of your Exchange account in the Mail, Contacts, Calendars screen; tapping Account Info; and flipping the SSL slider to On or Off, depending on how it should be configured.

5. When you're prompted to choose the kinds of data—Mail, Contacts, and Calendars—that you want to synchronize between your iPod and the Exchange server (**Figure 5.1**), flick the switch for those data types to On, and then tap Save.

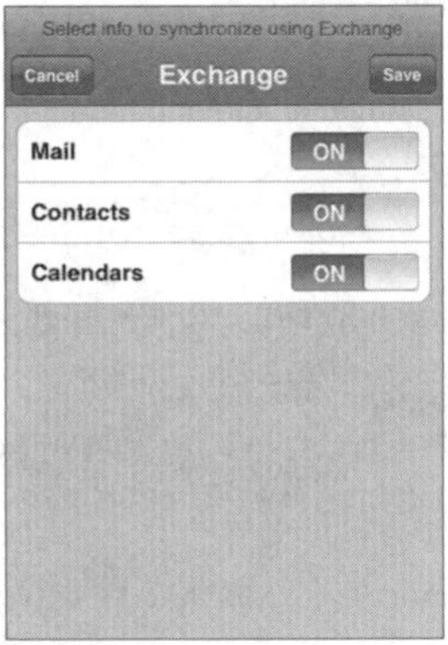

Figure 5.1
Choose the kind of data you want to sync with the Exchange server.

By default, the iPod synchronizes just 3 days' worth of email. If you need to store more email on your iPod, select your Exchange account in the Mail, Contacts, Calendars screen; tap Mail Days to Sync; and choose a new number of days' worth of email to synchronize. Your options are No Limit, 1 Day, 3 Days, 1 Week, 2 Weeks, and 1 Month.

note When you create an Exchange account on your iPod and choose to sync contacts and calendars, any existing contacts and calendars information on the iPod will be wiped out, replaced by contacts and events from the Exchange server. Additionally, you can't synchronize this kind of data via iTunes with your computer. You *can* synchronize data between your iPod and personal computer if you have a MobileMe account, however.

Configuring MobileMe, Gmail, Yahoo, and AOL accounts

The iPod's designers made configuring one of these accounts really easy. Just follow these steps:

1. Tap the Settings icon in the iPod's Home screen and then tap Mail, Contacts, Calendars.

2. Tap Add Account, and choose MobileMe, Gmail, Yahoo Mail, or AOL.

3. In the screen that appears, enter your name, the email address for this account, your account's password, and a descriptive name for the account—*My Mighty MobileMe Account*, for example.

4. Tap Save.

Unlike its practice with other kinds of accounts, the iPod doesn't demand settings for incoming and outgoing mail servers. It's intimately familiar with these services and does all that configuration for you. But you're welcome to muck with these more-arcane settings after you create the account, if you like (and I tell you how in the "Configuring further" section later in this chapter).

Configuring POP and IMAP accounts

If you're like a lot of people and have an email account through a "regular" Internet service provider (ISP) that provides email via a DSL or cable broadband connection, you'll configure your iPod this way:

1. Tap the Settings icon in the iPod's Home screen and then tap Mail, Contacts, Calendars.

2. Tap Add Account.

3. Tap Other.

   I ask you to tap Other because this option lets you set up email accounts for ISPs other than those listed above the Other entry. In the resulting screen, you have the option to add mail accounts (as well as server-based contacts and calendars, which I'll deal with later).

4. Tap Add Mail Account.

   In the resulting New Account screen, enter the information for setting up a POP or IMAP account.

5. Tap Name, and enter your real name (as opposed to your user name).

6. Tap Address, and enter your email address (such as *example@ examplemail.com*).

7. Tap Password, and enter the account's password.

8. Tap Description, and enter a description of your account.

   I often use the name of my account for this entry—*Macworld*, for example.

9. Tap Save to save your settings.

   The iPod looks up the account settings you've entered. If you've set up an account for a common email carrier—Cox or BellSouth, for example—it checks your account and configures the server settings for you.

If the iPod can't configure your account, or if the ISP offers IMAP and POP accounts and doesn't know which kind you have, the New Account screen displays new options.

10. Choose IMAP or POP.

   At the top of the screen, you see IMAP and POP buttons. Tap the button for the kind of account you have.

11. Enter the host name in the Incoming Mail Server area.

   This information, provided by your ISP, is in the format *mail. examplemail.com*.

12. Tap User Name, and enter the name that precedes the at (@) symbol in your email address.

   If the address is *bruno@examplemail.com*, for example, type **bruno**.

13. Tap Password, and enter the password for your email account.

> **note** Type the password very carefully. With the 2.0 and later software, password fields are a bit better about showing you what you've typed rather than displaying just black dots. When you enter a password character, the password field briefly displays the character you just typed—4 or W, for example. But the characters don't remain onscreen long, and you may miss them. Check your work before you lift your finger off the keyboard.

14. Below Outgoing Mail Server, tap Host Name; then enter the appropriate text—which, once again, will be provided by your ISP, typically in the format *smtp.examplemail.com*.

15. Enter your user name and password again, if required.

   If these fields aren't filled in for you, copy this information from the Incoming Mail Server area and paste it in here.

16. When you've double-checked to make sure everything's correct, tap Save in the top-right corner of the screen.

The configured account (**Figure 5.2**) appears in the list of accounts in the Mail Settings screen.

Figure 5.2
Configured email POP account.

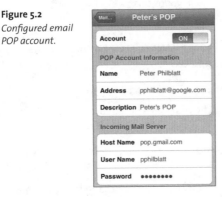

Configuring further

Most people can stop right here and get on with mucking with Mail, but your email account may require a little extra tweaking for it to work. Here's how to do just that:

1. Tap Settings in the Home screen; then tap Mail, Contacts, Calendars.

2. Tap your account name.

3. If you'd like that account to appear in Mail's Accounts list, be sure that the Account slider is set to On.

tip Why turn it off? Perhaps you've got a load of messages sitting on the server that you'd rather not download with your iPod. Download those messages with your computer, delete them from the server, and then enable the account on your iPod.

4. Verify that the information in the account's settings fields is correct; if not, tap the field you want to edit and start typing.

5. Tap the SMTP button to configure the outgoing server for your email account (see the nearby sidebar "Out and About" for more details).

6. Tap the Advanced button at the bottom of the screen, and in the resulting Advanced screen for POP accounts (**Figure 5.3** on the following page), choose the options you want.

Putting It on the IMAP

At one time, POP accounts—accounts that require you to download email to your computer to read it—were the norm. But increasingly, IMAP email accounts—those that store messages on an ISP's central server—are becoming more popular. In the case of the iPod touch, they should be, because using an IMAP account can help reduce clutter and confusion. Here's how.

Suppose that you have a POP account that's configured to download your email to both your computer and your iPod. You read the mail once on your iPod and delete it when you're done. A copy remains on your computer, though, so you have to delete it there too. You can avoid this double duty with an IMAP account, because IMAP email—living as it does on a central server out there in "the cloud"—can be managed by any device that can access it.

So you log on to your IMAP account with your iPod and peruse your email. You find some messages you don't want any longer, and you delete them. When you do, they vanish from the server. When you return home to your computer, you won't see those messages, because you've deleted them. Unlike with a POP account, the contents of your email are exactly the same, regardless of which device you use to read it.

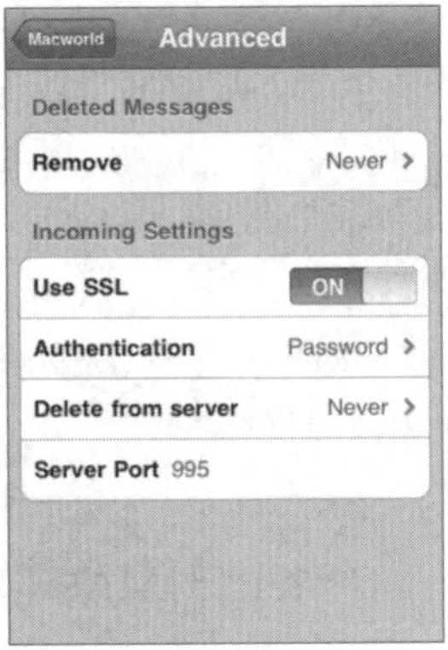

Figure 5.3
*A POP account's
Advanced
settings.*

Use these settings to specify

- The interval the iPod will wait before it removes deleted messages from its Trash. Options are Never, After One Day, After One Week, and After One Month

- Whether your account will use SSL protection to transmit and receive email

- The kind of authentication your account requires (MD5 Challenge-Response, NTLM, HTTP MD5 Digest, or Password)

- When you want email to be deleted from the server (options include Never, Seven Days, and When Removed from Inbox)

- The incoming server port for your account

  This information is individual enough that I'll leave it to your IT or ISP representative to tell you how to configure these options. Worth noting, however, is that you may be able to suss out these settings by looking at how the email client on your computer is configured.

  For IMAP accounts, you have some different options in the Advanced screen. You can choose which mailboxes will hold drafts, sent email, and deleted messages. You can choose when to remove deleted messages (Never, After One Day, After One Week, or After One Month). You can turn SSL on or off if the account isn't with Yahoo Mail, which doesn't offer an SSL option. You can choose the same authentication schemes as your POP-using sisters and brothers. You can enter an IMAP path prefix—a path name required by some IMAP servers so that they can show folders properly. And you can change the incoming server port.

Out and About

The iPod touch 2.0 and later software is very smart about sending email. It works like this:

In the old days, you'd configure your email account with a particular SMTP server. If you took your iPod touch on the road, and that SMTP server didn't work, you were stuck with an email message in the outbox that wouldn't send. This problem usually happened because of an antispam measure: The network you were connected to (in a coffee shop or hotel, for example) didn't allow messages to be relayed from one ISP's SMTP server through another's SMTP server.

This "no relaying" policy hasn't changed at all. What *has* changed is the iPod's flexibility. Now, just select an account in the Mail, Contacts, Calendars screen and tap the SMTP button, and you'll see a list of all the SMTP servers your iPod has settings for. At the top of the list is the primary server—the server address you entered (or that was entered for you) when you created the account. Next to this server's name is the word *On*.

Below the primary server is the Other SMTP Servers entry, listing all other SMTP servers your iPod believes that it can access. By default, these entries have the word *Off* after their names. Tap one (a Gmail

(continued on next page)

Out and About (continued)

server, for example), and in the resulting screen, you have the option to turn that server on. When you do, if the iPod is prevented from sending messages from the primary server, it tries to send from one of the other servers that you've enabled.

This feature alone justifies getting a free Gmail or Yahoo account, as public Wi-Fi hotspots rarely block mail sent through Gmail's or Yahoo's SMTP servers.

One other SMTP option, while we're here: If you need to change the SMTP server port from the default setting of 25, you do it by tapping an SMTP server in the SMTP screen, tapping the Server Port entry at the bottom of the screen, and then typing a new value with the onscreen numeric keyboard that appears. Why do it? Many ISPs provide an SMTP server port (usually, 587) that can be relayed through other SMTP servers. If you find that your iPod can't send a message, try changing your email account's SMTP port to 587 or to the public port number provided by your ISP.

Understanding Mail, Contacts, Calendars behavior

Before I leave the Mail, Contacts, Calendar screen, I should examine the options that tell the Mail, Contacts, and Calendars applications how to behave (**Figure 5.4**).

View the bottom part of the screen, and you find these options below the Mail heading:

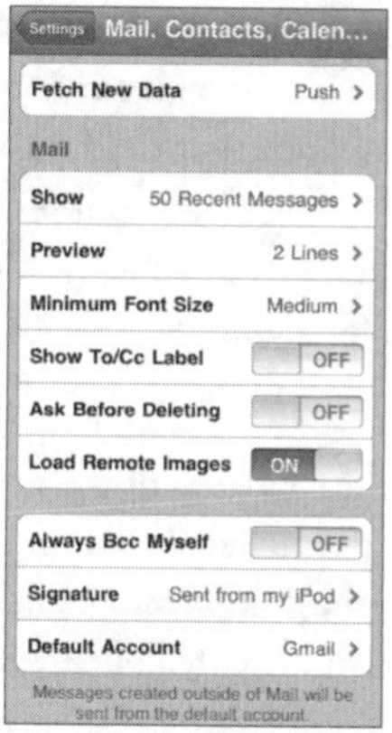

Figure 5.4
Additional Mail settings.

Settings   Mail, Contacts, Calen...
Fetch New Data   Push >
Mail
Show   50 Recent Messages >
Preview   2 Lines >
Minimum Font Size   Medium >
Show To/Cc Label   OFF
Ask Before Deleting   OFF
Load Remote Images   ON
Always Bcc Myself   OFF
Signature   Sent from my iPod >
Default Account   Gmail >
Messages created outside of Mail will be sent from the default account.

Fetch New Data. Thanks to the iPod 2.0 and later software's Microsoft Exchange and MobileMe support, new data such as events, contacts, and email can be transferred (or *pushed*) to your iPod automatically. You don't have to tell the iPod to retrieve this data; retrieval just happens. When you tap Fetch New Data, you're taken to the screen of the same name, where you can switch off Push (**Figure 5.5**).

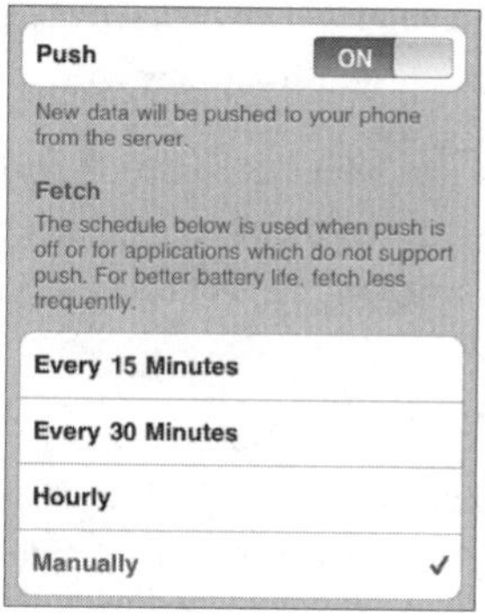

Figure 5.5
The Fetch New Data screen.

Push   ON
New data will be pushed to your phone from the server.
Fetch
The schedule below is used when push is off or for applications which do not support push. For better battery life, fetch less frequently.
Every 15 Minutes
Every 30 Minutes
Hourly
Manually   ✓

Additionally, you find Fetch settings here. Fetch is essentially a scheduler for your iPod; it tells the device how often to go out and get information such as email messages from an account that can't push email, such as a POP account. (Fetch can also retrieve data from services such as MobileMe and Yahoo that push data but for which you've turned push off.) You can configure the iPod to fetch data every 15 or 30 minutes, hourly, or manually.

If you tap the Advanced button at the bottom of the window, you're taken to an Advanced screen, where you can determine how your various email accounts behave with regard to pushing and fetching. You can configure a MobileMe or Yahoo account with a Push, Fetch, or Manual option, for example. Accounts that don't support push can be configured only for Fetch or Manual.

> **tip** Pushing and fetching burn through a battery charge faster than using a manual setting, because your iPod has to perform battery-draining tasks such as logging onto servers to retrieve data. Fetch demands more from a battery than push does. For this reason, if you need to be miserly with your battery, fetch less often and turn push off.

Show. How many messages would you like Mail to display? Options include 25, 50, 75, 100, and 200 recent messages.

Preview. When you view message subjects within a mailbox in one of your Mail accounts, you see the first bit of text in each message. The Preview entry determines how many lines of this text you'll see: none, 1, 2, 3, 4, or 5 lines.

Minimum Font Size. This setting determines how large the text will be in your email messages: Small, Medium, Large, Extra Large, or Giant. Medium is good for most eyes, and it saves a lot of scrolling.

Show To/Cc Label. When this option is set to on, Mail plasters a *To* next to messages that were sent directly to you and a *Cc* next to messages on which you were copied.

Ask Before Deleting. When you turn this option on, if you tap the Trash icon to delete the message you're reading, you'll be asked to confirm your decision. If you swipe a message and then tap the red Delete icon that appears or use the iPod's bulk-delete option, however, you won't be asked for confirmation.

Load Remote Images. Like the email client on your computer, the iPod is capable of automatically showing you images embedded in messages. By default, this option is on.

Always Bcc Myself. If you're the kind of person who wants a copy of every message you send (but don't want the recipients of those messages to know), switch on this option. You'll get your copies.

Signature. Ever wonder where that proud *Sent from My iPod* message comes from—the one that appears at the bottom of every message you send from your iPod? Right here. As a new iPod owner, you'll want to stick with this default message for a while, simply for the bragging rights. Feel free to tap this option later and enter some pithy signoff of your own.

Default Account. If you have more than one email account set up, this setting determines which account will send images, notes, and other links. When you send one of these items, you can't choose which account sends it, so give this option some thought. You may discover that Wi-Fi hotspots are reluctant to send mail through your regular ISP's SMTP server, whereas Gmail accounts rarely have this problem. For this reason, you may want to make your Gmail account the default.

These Contacts settings appear next (**Figure 5.6**):

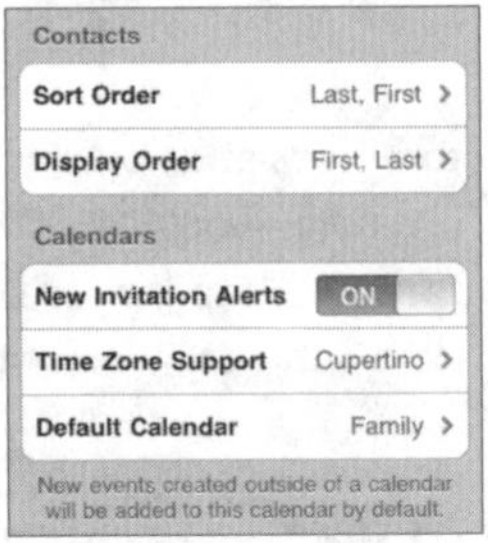

Figure 5.6
*Additional
Contacts and
Calendar settings.*

Contacts	
Sort Order	Last, First >
Display Order	First, Last >
Calendars	
New Invitation Alerts	ON
Time Zone Support	Cupertino >
Default Calendar	Family >

New events created outside of a calendar
will be added to this calendar by default.

Sort Order. Tap this option to choose between sorting contacts by First, Last name or by Last, First name.

Display Order. Similar to Sort Order, this option lets you display your contacts as either First, Last or Last, First.

Finally, you see these Calendar settings at the bottom of the screen:

New Invitation Alerts. This On/Off switch lets you view—or not—meeting invitations you've received (those pushed to you from an Exchange server, for example).

Time Zone Support. Tap this command, and you're taken to the Time Zone Support screen, where you can turn Time Zone Support on or off. Below that setting is an option to choose the time zone of a major city.

When Time Zone Support is on, Calendar's events are shown in the time of the selected city. So, for example, you could choose London even if you're in San Francisco and see events in London time. Switch this option off, and events are shown in the iPod's current location (which is determined by network time).

Default Calendar. Tap this command to choose a calendar where the iPod will add events created outside the Calendar application.

Sending and Receiving Mail

Now that your accounts are *finally* set up properly, you can send and receive messages. The process works this way.

Receiving email

Receiving email is dead simple. Just follow these steps:

1. Tap the Mail icon in the iPod's Home screen.

   Mail will check for new messages when you first launch the application. If you have new messages, the iPod will download them.

   When it does, a number appears next to the account name, indicating the account's number of unread messages. Any messages that contain attachments bear a paper-clip icon next to the sender's name.

2. Tap the account name.

   You'll see a list of that account's mailboxes. For POP accounts, those mailboxes include Inbox, Drafts (if you've saved any composed messages without sending them), Sent (if you've sent any messages from that account), and Trash (if you've deleted any messages from that account). For IMAP accounts, you'll most likely see Inbox, Drafts, Sent, Trash, and any folders associated with the account—folders that you've added to a MobileMe or Google account, for example.

   These folder names, however, depend entirely on what the host service calls them. Gmail, for example, gathers the messages you've sent into the Sent Mail folder (**Figure 5.7** on the following page).

   In the bottom-right corner of an account screen, you'll see a Compose icon. Tap it, and a New Message screen appears, along with the iPod's keyboard. I talk about creating new messages in "Creating and sending email" later in this chapter.

Figure 5.7
An account screen.

3. Tap the Inbox.

   Messages appear in a list, with the most recently received messages at the top. Unread messages have a blue dot next to them. The Inbox heading will have a number in parentheses next to it—*Inbox (22)*, for example. That *(22)* means that you have 22 unread messages.

   This screen also bears a Compose icon and, in the bottom-left corner, a Retrieve icon, which you tap to check for new mail.

   An Edit button in the top-right corner lets you delete messages. Tap it, and all the messages in the list acquire a dim gray circle next to them. This circle is for marking messages that you want to delete or move. Tap one of these circles, and a red check icon appears within it. Continue tapping messages until you've selected all the messages you'd like to delete or move. Then tap the Delete button at the bottom of the screen, and all the messages will be moved to the Trash. (Alternatively, with regard to deleting messages, you can do without the Edit button. Swipe your finger across a message entry to force a Delete button to appear, and tap Delete; the message moves to the Trash.)

Tap Move, and a Mailboxes screen scrolls up from the bottom, listing all available mailboxes for that account. Choose a mailbox, and the selected messages move to it. This move feature is really useful only if you're using an IMAP account, as unlike POP accounts, IMAP accounts can have additional folders for filing email messages.

note When you delete a message, it's not really gone; it's simply moved to the Trash mailbox. To delete the message for real, you can either wait out the remove interval listed in the account's Mail setting (see "Configuring further" earlier in this chapter) or tap Trash. Then you can swipe a message and tap the Delete button that appears next to the message; tap Edit and then tap Delete All at the bottom of the screen; or cherry-pick the messages you want to delete by tapping the gray circles next to them and then tapping the Delete (#) button (where # equals the number of messages you've selected). Then—and only then—is a message truly gone.

Spam and the iPod

As I write these words, the iPod touch's Mail application lacks a *spam filter*—a utility that looks through your incoming email for junk mail and quarantines it in a special mailbox. This lack is a drag if you're using an account that attracts a lot of spam.

My solution? Don't use such an account on your iPod. Google offers its free Gmail email service at www.gmail.com. Gmail provides loads of email storage (probably more than your current ISP does), and you can access it from the Web, your iPod, and your computer's email client. Best of all, it offers excellent spam filtering. Additionally, you can set up Gmail so that your other mail accounts are forwarded to it. This setup allows Gmail to filter spam from these accounts too before the mail is delivered to your inbox. Like I said, it's free. Give it a try.

Navigating the Message screen

Simple though it may be, the Message screen packs a punch. In it, you find not only standard email elements such as From and To fields, Subject, and message body, but also icons for adding contacts and for filing, trashing, replying to, and forwarding messages. The screen breaks down this way.

Before the body

The top of the Message screen displays the number of messages in the mailbox as well as the number of the displayed message—*2 of 25*, for example. Tap the up or down arrow to the right to move quickly to the previous or next message in the mailbox (**Figure 5.8**).

Figure 5.8
Message body with document attached.

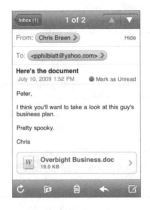

Below that, you'll see From and To fields. Each field will display at least one contact name or email address (one of which could be your own) in a blue bubble. Tap one of these bubbles, and if the name or address is in your iPod's Contacts directory, you'll be taken to its owner's Info screen. If the name or address isn't among your contacts, a screen will appear, offering you the hidden option of emailing the person, creating a new contact or adding the address to an existing Contacts entry (**Figure 5.9**).

Figure 5.9
An unknown contact's Info screen.

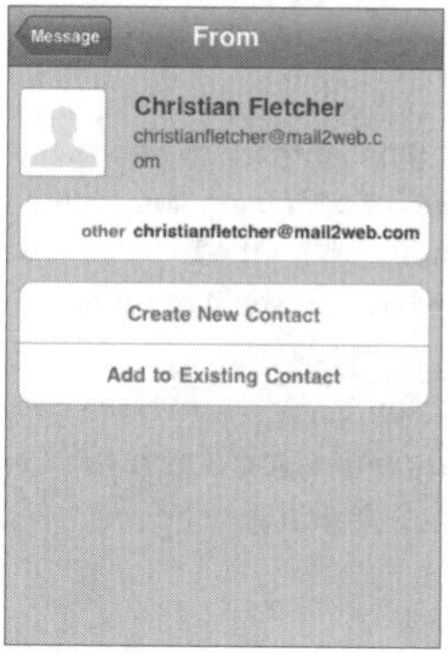

Hidden option? Yes. That person's email address is listed next to the Other heading. Tap that email address, and a new email message opens with that person's address in the To field. The email will be sent from the account you're currently working in.

Tap Create New Contact, and a New Contact screen appears, with that person's name at the top and his email address filled in below. If the message has no name associated with it—if you were sent a message from a company address such as *info@example.com*, for example—no name will appear in the Name field.

Tap Add to Existing Contact, and a list of all the contacts on your iPod appears. Tap a contact, and the address is added to that contact. If you'd like to edit the contact—indicate that the address belongs to Home or Work, for example—tap the blue bubble again to bring up the contact's Info screen, tap the Edit button, tap the email address to produce the Edit Email screen, tap Other, and choose a different label in the Label screen.

You can hide the To field by tapping the Hide entry near it. This action hides all the To fields in all the messages in all your accounts, and it changes the Hide entry to Details. To expose the To fields again, just tap Details.

> **tip** Hiding the To field can be really helpful when someone insists on filling To fields with dozens of addresses (something that's considered to be both rude and a privacy violation). With the To field hidden, you can see the beginning of the message immediately instead of countless addresses.

Below the From and To fields, you'll see the message subject, followed by the date. If you have details showing, you'll also see a Mark As Unread entry. Tap this entry to do exactly what it suggests.

Body talk

Finally, in the area below, are the pithy words you've been waiting for. Just as in your computer's email client, you'll see the text of the message. Quoted text appears with a vertical line to its left—or more than one line, depending on how many quote "layers" the message has. If a message has several quote layers, each vertical line is a different color. (The first three layers are blue, green, and red, respectively; subsequent layers are red from there on out.)

If the message has attachments, they will appear below the message text. If Cousin Bill sends photos from his latest vacation, they'll appear here (**Figure 5.10**).

URLs and email addresses contained within messages appear as blue, live links. Tap a URL, and Safari launches and takes you to that Web page. (I cover Safari in Chapter 6.) Tap an email address, and a new email message opens with that address in the To field.

Figure 5.10
*Message with
attached photo.*

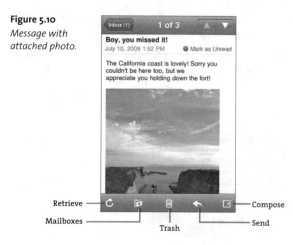

Retrieve ——————— Compose

Mailboxes ——————— Send

Trash

> **tip** The iPod is smart about URLs. Both http://www.example.com
> and www.example.com appear as live links, for example, but
> example.com does not.

The tools below

The toolbar at the bottom of the screen contains five icons (refer to
Figure 5.10):

Retrieve. Tap this circular icon, and the iPod will check for new messages
for that account.

Mailboxes. When you tap the Mailboxes icon, you're presented with a
list of all the mailboxes associated with that account. Tap one of these
mailboxes, and the message will be filed there. (Use this method to move
a message out of the Trash.)

Trash. Tap this icon, and the cute little trash can pops its top and sucks the message into it. Like I said, to move messages out of the Trash, just tap the Trash mailbox in your account screen, tap a message, tap the Mailboxes icon, and then tap the mailbox where you'd like to put the message.

Send. The left-arrow icon is your pathway to the Reply, Reply All, Forward, and Save Image commands (**Figure 5.11**).

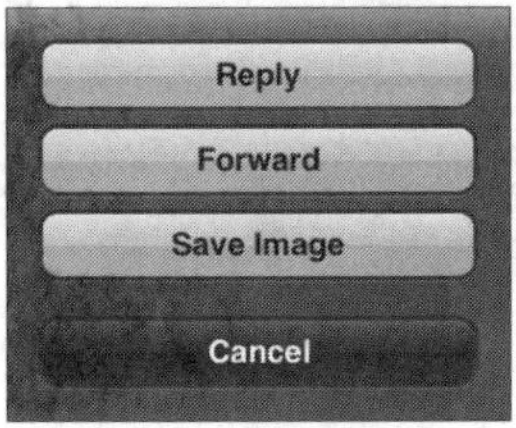

Figure 5.11
The Reply sheet.

When you tap the Send icon and then the Reply button that appears, a new message appears, with the Subject heading *Re: Original Message Subject,* in which *Original Message Subject* is . . . well, you know. The message is addressed to the sender of the original message, and the insertion point awaits at the top of the message body. The original text is quoted below. The message is mailed from the account you're working in.

If a message you received was sent to multiple recipients, tapping Reply All lets you reply to all the recipients of the original message.

Tap Forward, and you're responsible for filling in the To field in the resulting message. You can type it yourself with the keyboard that appears or tap the plus (+) icon to add a recipient from your iPod's list of contacts. This message bears *Fwd:* at the beginning of the Subject heading, followed by the original heading. The original message's From and To information appear at the top of the message as quoted text followed by the original message.

Finally, if a message has images attached to it, you'll see a Save *X* Images button, where *X* is the number of images. (The button will read Save Image if there's just one image.) Tap that button, and the attached images will be added to the Saved Photos collection in the Photos application.

Compose. Last is your old friend the Compose icon. Tap it, and a New Message screen appears, ready for your input.

Creating and sending email

If it truly is better to give than receive, the following instructions for composing and delivering mail from your iPod should enrich your life significantly. With regard to email, the iPod can give nearly as good as it gets. Here's how to go about it.

As I mention earlier in the chapter, you can create new email messages by tapping the Compose icon that appears in every account and mailbox screen. You'll even find the Compose icon available when you've selected Trash. To create a message, follow these steps:

1. Tap the Compose icon.

   By default, Mail fills the From field with the address for this account. But you needn't use that account. Just tap From, and any other email accounts you have will appear in a scrolling list. Tap the one you want.

2. In the New Message screen that appears, type the recipient's email address, or in the To field, tap the plus icon.

   When you place the insertion point in the To or Cc/Bcc field, notice that the iPod's keyboard adds @ and period (.) characters where the spacebar usually resides. (The spacebar is still there; it's just smaller.) This feature makes typing addresses easier because you don't have to switch to the numbers-and-symbols keyboard.

Tap and hold the period key, and—good gosh almighty!—.net, .edu, .org, and .com pop up as part of a contextual menu. How handy is that?

When you start typing a name, the iPod will suggest recipients based on entries in your list of contacts (**Figure 5.12**). If the recipient you want appears in the list below the To field, tap that name to add it to the field.

Figure 5.12
Begin typing to find a contact.

When you tap the plus icon, your list of contacts appears. Navigate through your contacts, and tap the one you want to add to the To field. Some contacts will have multiple email addresses; tap the one you'd like to use. To add more names to the To field, type them or tap the plus icon to add them.

To delete a recipient, tap that contact and then tap the Delete key on the iPod's keyboard.

3. If you'd like to Cc or Bcc someone, tap in that field, tap in the appropriate field—CC or Bcc—and then use any of the techniques in step 2 for adding a recipient.

4. Tap the Subject field, and enter a subject for your message with the iPod's keyboard.

   That subject replaces *New Message* at the top of the screen.

5. Tap in the message body (or, if the insertion point is in the Subject field, tap Return on the iPod's keyboard to move to the message body), and type your message.

6. Tap Send to send the message or Cancel to save or delete your message.

   The Send icon, in the top-right corner, is easy enough to understand. Tap that icon, and the message is sent from the current account. You'll know that it's been sent when you hear a swoosh sound.

   Cancel is a little more confusing. If you've typed anywhere in the To field, New Message screen's Subject field, or message body (even if you subsequently deleted everything you typed), a sheet will roll up when you tap Cancel, displaying Save, Don't Save, and Cancel icons. Tap Save to store the message in the account's Drafts mailbox. (If no such mailbox exists, the iPod will create one.) When you tap Don't Save, the message is deleted. When you tap Cancel, the iPod assumes that you made a mistake when you tapped Cancel the first time, and it removes this sheet.

   If the iPod can't send a message—when you don't have access to a Wi-Fi network—it creates an Outbox for the account from which you're trying to send the message. When you next use Mail and are able to send the message, the iPod will make the connection and send any messages in the Outbox, at which point the Outbox will disappear.

Working with pushy MobileMe

Apple's $100-per-annum MobileMe Web service does a lot of things: provides 20 GB of online storage; gives you a place to post galleries of images and videos; and offers Webcentric mail, calendar, and contacts applications. For purposes of this discussion, one of the most important things it does is automatically synchronize (or *push*) mail, contact, calendar, and Internet bookmark information among your computers, your iPod touch, and Apple's Internet-based MobileMe server. So, for example, when you enter a new event in the iPod's Calendar application, it also soon appears within MobileMe's Calendar component on the Web, as well as on any computer that's synced with MobileMe. You set it up this way.

Configuring MobileMe on the Macintosh

You configure MobileMe through the MobileMe system preference, as follows:

1. Choose Apple > System Preferences.

2. Click the MobileMe preference in the Internet & Network section and then click the Sync tab.

3. Check the Synchronize with MobileMe box, and choose Automatically from the pop-up menu.

   When you choose Automatically, you enable MobileMe's push capabilities. This command tells MobileMe that when some new data is added to the MobileMe Web site or to your iPod (you've uploaded a photo to a photo gallery, created a new calendar event, or added a new contact, for example), that data should be pushed almost immediately to the other devices synced with your MobileMe account.

   Note that this is not the case with data created on your computer. When you choose Automatically from this pop-up menu on your computer, any new data you create will be synchronized every 15 minutes. If you need that data synced sooner, simply click the Sync Now button.

4. In the Sync tab's scrolling pane, select the kind of data you'd like to synchronize.

You'll see several options in this pane, but the ones you're concerned about here are Calendars and Contacts (**Figure 5.13**).

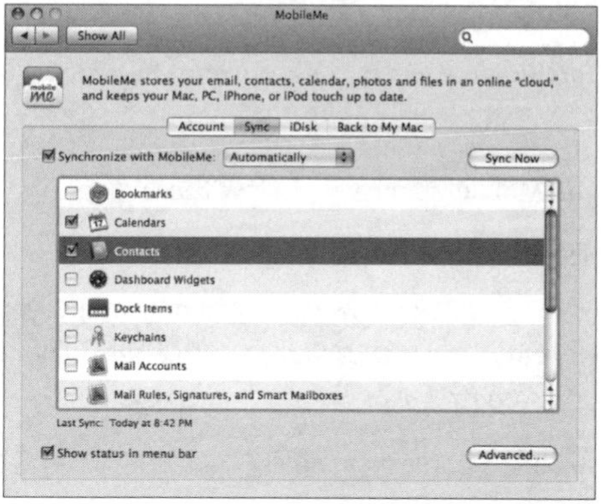

Figure 5.13
*A Mac's
MobileMe system
preference.*

5. To synchronize this data with MobileMe immediately, click Sync Now.

In the process, you may see a dialog box that asks how you'd like to sync your data. The options include merging your computer and MobileMe data, replacing the data on your computer with MobileMe's data, or replacing MobileMe's data with the data on your computer.

If you click the More Options button, you can choose a different option for the kinds of data you're syncing. You can choose to merge contacts but replace the calendars on your Mac with MobileMe's calendar information, for example.

Your Mac will do as you ask and synchronize your data. If the synchronization was successful, and if you chose to sync calendars and contacts, you should see the same data in iCal and Address Book that is available on the MobileMe Web site.

Configuring MobileMe in Windows

The process of syncing your data with MobileMe in Windows is similar to the Macintosh experience. The difference is that MobileMe syncs with Windows applications such as Microsoft Outlook and Windows Contacts, because Apple's iCal and Address Book don't come in Windows versions.

note For this procedure to work, you must have iTunes 8.2 or later and, of course, a MobileMe account.

To configure MobileMe on a PC, follow these steps:

1. Download and install MobileMe Setup.

   If you don't have MobileMe installed on your PC, you'll have to get it from http://support.apple.com/downloads/MobileMe_Control_Panel_for_Windows.

2. Choose Start > Control Panels.

3. Open the MobileMe Preferences control panel, sign in with your MobileMe user name and password, and click the Sync tab.

4. Enable the Sync with MobileMe option, and choose Automatically from the pop-up menu.

   (See the Macintosh configuration information in the preceding section to find out why you choose Automatically.)

5. Enable the kinds of data you want to sync.

   Your choices are Contacts, Calendars, and Bookmarks. When you choose Contacts, you can sync with Outlook, Google Contacts, Yahoo Address Book, and Windows Contacts. For Calendars, you can sync only with Outlook. And Bookmarks can be synced with Internet Explorer or the Windows version of Apple's Web browser, Safari (see Chapter 6).

6. Click Sync Now.

   As with Macintosh syncing, you'll be asked how you'd like to have the sync performed. Here, too, you can choose how particular kinds of data are synced.

Configuring the iPod

Now that your computer is configured, you're ready to add the iPod to the mix, as follows:

1. Tap Settings and then tap Mail, Contacts, Calendars.

2. In the Accounts area, tap your MobileMe account.

3. In the account screen that appears, switch on those data types you'd like to sync with MobileMe.

   Your choices are Mail, Contacts, Calendars, and Bookmarks (**Figure 5.14**). Contacts, calendars, and bookmarks work as I describe earlier in this chapter; when contacts and calendar items are created, they're synchronized with MobileMe and any computers linked to your MobileMe account.

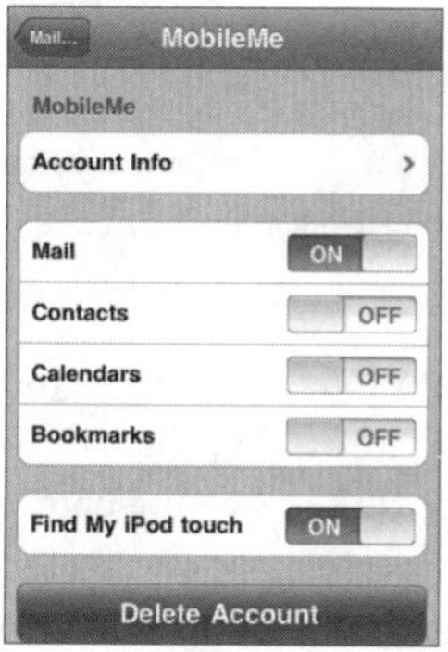

Figure 5.14
The iPod touch's MobileMe syncing options.

When you switch on the Mail option, however, you're telling MobileMe to send any received messages to your iPod immediately. When the Mail option is switched off, you'll receive that mail only when you launch the Mail application and check for it.

note When you enable MobileMe syncing for bookmarks, contacts, or calendars, the syncing option for those enabled data types will no longer be available for the iPod in iTunes.

Below the syncing options, you see the Find My iPod touch switch. This service, exclusive to MobileMe members, can help you track down a missing iPod. I describe its workings in Chapter 9.

Managing Contacts

The Contacts application is important for a couple of reasons. Not only is it the place to look when you need a quick address or phone number, but it also interacts with other iPod touch applications, including Mail, Calendar, and Maps. For these reasons, you'll want to know your way around Contacts. You soon will.

Entering the people you know

Tap the Home screen's Contacts application, and you see a list of your contacts in alphabetical order (**Figure 5.15**) and, above that, a Search field for seeking out contacts.

This list works very much like any long list of items you see in the iPod's Music area. A tiny alphabet runs down the right side of the screen. Tap a letter to move immediately to contacts whose names (first or last, depending on how you've configured name sorting in the Mail, Contacts, Calendars preferences) begin with this letter. Alternatively, tap in the

Search field, and when the iPod's keyboard swoops up from the bottom of the screen, start typing some letters in your contact's name. As you type, fewer names appear as the choices narrow.

Figure 5.15
The Contacts screen.

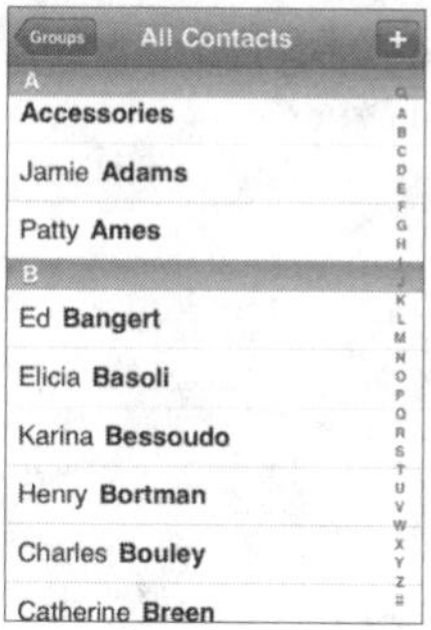

When you tap a name, you're taken to that contact's Info screen (**Figure 5.16**). Here, you can find information including the following:

Figure 5.16
A contact's Info screen.

- Photo

  This item can be a photo you've added in Address Book on a Mac, by tapping Add Photo and choosing a picture from your Photos collection, or by assigning a picture to a contact in the Photos Camera application.

- Name
- Company
- Phone number

  Possible phone headings include Mobile, iPod, Home, Work, Main, Home Fax, Work Fax, Pager, and Other.

- Ringtone
- Email address

  This item includes Home, Work, and Other options, as well as any custom labels you've created.

- URL (for the contact's Web site)
- Home address
- Work address
- Other address
- Other fields

You won't necessarily find all these entries in a contact's Info screen; this list just shows you what's possible to include.

Organizing contacts in groups

Although you see a list of all your contacts when you first tap Contacts, the Contacts application has an organizational layer above the main list. If, in the iPod touch's Info preference within iTunes, you've chosen to sync your address book with select groups of contacts, or if your full address book contains groups of contacts, those groups will appear in the Groups screen, which you access by tapping the Groups button in the top-left corner of the Contacts screen (**Figure 5.17**).

Figure 5.17
*The Groups
screen.*

Groups	
All Contacts	>
Breen family	>
Favorites	>
System 9	>
With Phone	>

Organizing in groups makes a lot of sense if you have loads of contacts. Although Apple made traversing a long list of contacts as easy as possible, easier still is tapping something like a Family group and picking Uncle Bud's name out of a list of 17 beloved relatives.

Feelin' Groupy

I've found it really helpful to create a group that includes just contacts that have email addresses. It makes a lot of sense to include these contacts because you can email them from your iPod touch.

In Apple's Address Book, you can create just such a group easily. Choose File > New Smart Group, and configure the resulting pane to read Contains Cards Which Match the Following Conditions: Email Is Set. This step places all contacts that contain an email address in their own group. Then you can sync this group to your iPod so that you don't have to bother trying to email contacts you don't have this information for.

Regrettably, iPod-compatible Windows applications (Outlook, Outlook Express, and Windows' Address Book) with address-book functionality don't have this kind of easy-does-it feature.

Making contacts

The best way to become familiar with the iPod's contacts is to make some of your own. To do that now, tap Contacts and then the plus icon in the top-right corner of the iPod's screen.

Viewing the New Contact screen

The New Contact screen contains fields for the elements I list in "Entering the people you know" earlier in this chapter—photo, first and last name, phone numbers, email addresses, URL, physical addresses (Home, Work, and Other, for example)—as well as an Add Field entry (**Figure 5.18**). To add information to one of these fields, tap the field or the green plus icon to its left. In the resulting screen, you'll find a place to enter the information.

Figure 5.18
The New Contact screen.

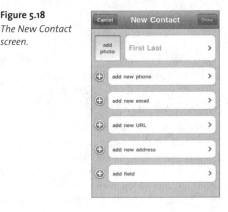

Here are the special features of each screen:

Add Photo. Tap this entry to display a sheet containing buttons marked Choose Existing Photo and Cancel. When you tap Choose Existing Photo, you're taken to your Photo Albums library, where you can select a picture.

You can move and scale these images by pinching, stretching, and dragging, and then tap Choose to attach them to the contact.

Name. In this screen, you enter first, last, and company names. Tap Save to return to the New Contact screen.

Add New Phone. As the name says, this field is where you add a phone number. In the Edit Phone screen, you tap in the number from the keypad and then choose the kind of phone number: Mobile, iPhone, Home, Work, Main, Home Fax, Work Fax, Pager, or Other. If you've added any custom labels within the iPod, Apple's Address Book (Mac), or Outlook (Windows), those custom labels will appear below these entries. At the very bottom, you'll find an Add Custom Label button that, when tapped, lets you type a label of your own making—*Dirigible* or *Private Train Car*, for example.

note The numeric keypad contains a key that reads +*#. Tap it, and these three characters appear on the keypad's bottom three keys, along with the word *pause*, which enters a comma (,) character. What good are these things? Automated answering systems use them for performing certain functions. Some phone systems, for example, require you to press the pound key and then a key combination to unblock a hidden phone number or append an extension. The comma character is commonly used to insert a 1-second delay. It's useful when an automated answering service demands that you wait a second before punching in another string of numbers. You can't make a call with your iPod touch as you can with an iPhone, of course, but this information will give you a clue about using such characters when you *are* talking on a phone.

Add New Email. Enter your contact's email addresses here. The iPod's keyboard in this screen contains @ and period (.) keys to make the process easier. Tap and hold the period key, and a menu appears that contains .net, .edu, .org, and .com. Just slide your finger over to the extension you want, and let go to enter it.

Add New URL. Similar idea here. The more-convenient keyboard is in evidence, but instead of an @ symbol, you'll find period (.), slash (/), and .com. You can apply a Home Page, Home, Work, or Other label to the URL, as well as any custom labels on your iPod.

Add New Address. In the United States, the default Edit Address screen contains two Street fields and areas for City, State, and Zip. Ah, but tap the country button and choose a different nation from the list that appears (these lists are divided into geographic regions such as Europe and Oceana), and these fields change. If you choose Belarus, for example, the bottom fields change to Postal Code, City, and Province. Tap the Label button next to the Country button to choose the nature of this address: Home, Work, Other, or (as you might expect) one of those custom labels.

Add Field. Tap Add Field, and you can add more fields to a contact's Info screen. These fields include Prefix, Phonetic First Name, Phonetic Last Name, Middle Name, Suffix, Nickname, Job Title, Department, Instant Message, Birthday, Date (Anniversary and Other are the options), and Note. Both the Birthday and Date screens contain the iPod's spinning date wheel for selecting the month, day, and year quickly.

Working with existing contacts

When you have contacts on your iPod, you can delete them, edit the information that they contain, or use that information to perform other tasks on your iPod.

To delete a contact, just tap the Edit icon that appears in the contact's Info screen, scroll to the bottom of the screen, and tap the big red Delete Contact button. You'll be asked to confirm your choice.

To edit a contact, tap that same Edit icon in the contact's Info screen, and make the edits you want (**Figure 5.19**). You can add information by tapping a field that begins with the word *Add* (or just tap its green plus icon). To delete information, tap the red minus (–) icon next to the information and then tap the now-revealed Delete button. When you're finished editing the contact, tap Done.

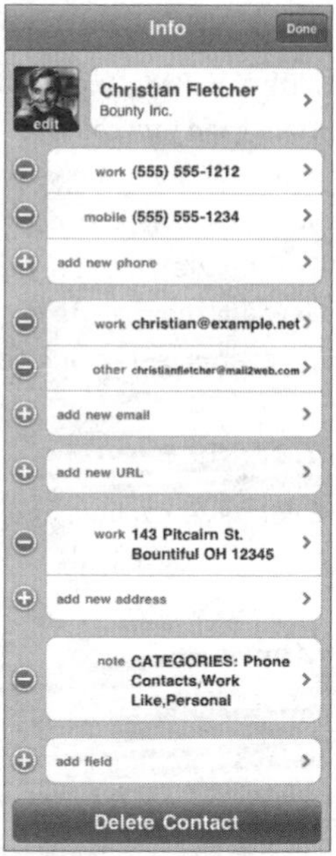

As for initiating actions on your iPod via a contact's Info screen, most of the elements in the screen are *live,* meaning that if you tap them, something happens. If you tap an email address, a New Message window appears in the Mail application, addressed to that person. If you tap a URL, Safari opens and takes you to that Web page. Tap an address, and Maps opens to show you its location.

At the bottom of an Info screen, you'll find a Share Contact button. Tap it to create a new email message that contains that person's contact information in the form of a vCard (a cross-platform file type that can be read on all computers and most devices that use contacts).

Figure 5.19
An elongated view of the contact edit screen.

Using Calendar

In the old days, the only way to get events on the iPod's calendar was to either type them on the device or sync the iPod with iTunes and ask it to copy your events from computer to iPod. Thanks to the introduction of Exchange and MobileMe push synchronization, the iPod's Calendar is a smarter application than it once was. In this section, I look at all the ways you can put life's events on your iPod.

Managing many calendars

With the iPod 2.0 and later software, the Calendar application can display more than one calendar—but it won't when you first launch the application. Instead, it shows your default calendar, as you configured it in the Mail, Contacts, Calendar setting. To view a list of all the calendars on your iPod, just tap the Calendars icon in the top-left corner of the screen. To view another calendar, tap that calendar's name. Or view all your calendar events by tapping the All entry.

Viewing events

Calendar is capable of displaying events in three views: List, Day, and Month. They're laid out like so.

Month

Tap Calendar, and by default, you'll see this month's calendar, with today's date highlighted in blue. Other days maintain a gray, businesslike appearance. Tap another day, and it adopts the blue box, while the present day gains a deeper gray hue. To return to the current day, either tap it (if you're viewing the current month) or tap the Today button in the bottom-left corner of the screen. To move to the next or previous month, tap the Previous or Next arrow, respectively, next to the month heading. To scan ahead more quickly, tap and hold one of these arrows.

Any days on the calendar that have events appended to them bear a small black dot below the date. Tap a day with a dot, and the events for that day appear in a list below the calendar (**Figure 5.20**), each preceded by its start time and colored dot, indicating the calendar to which the event is attached. (Each calendar is color-coded.) Tap an event in this list, and you're taken to the Event screen, which details the name and location of the event, its date, its start and end times, any alerts you've created, and any notes you've added to the event.

Figure 5.20
Month view with two events.

To edit or delete the event, tap the Edit icon in the top-right corner of the screen. Within the Edit screen, tap one of the fields to change its information. (I discuss these fields in "Creating events" later in this chapter.) To delete an event, tap the red Delete Event button at the bottom of the screen; then tap the Delete Event confirmation icon that appears.

Day

Tap the Day view button, and as you'd expect, you see the day laid out in a list, separated by hours. The day of the week and its date appear near the top of the screen. To move to the previous or next day, tap the Previous or Next arrow, respectively. To scan back or forward more quickly, tap and hold the appropriate arrow.

Events appear as colored bars (again, each calendar is color-coded, and that coding is reflected here) in the times they occupy and are labeled with the name of the appointment and its location (**Figure 5.21** on the following page). Just as you do with events in Month view, tap them to reveal their details; to edit them, tap the Edit button.

Figure 5.21
*Day view with
two events.*

List

List view shows a list of all the events on your calendar, separated by gray
date bars. Each gray bar bears the day's abbreviated name (*Fri* or *Mon*,
for example) and the month, date, and year of the event. The event's title
appears just below, preceded by its start time and colored dot indicating
its calendar association. Once again, tap an event to view its details. Tap
Edit to edit the event or delete it via the Delete Event button (**Figure 5.22**).
List is the single view that provides a Search field for finding events quickly.

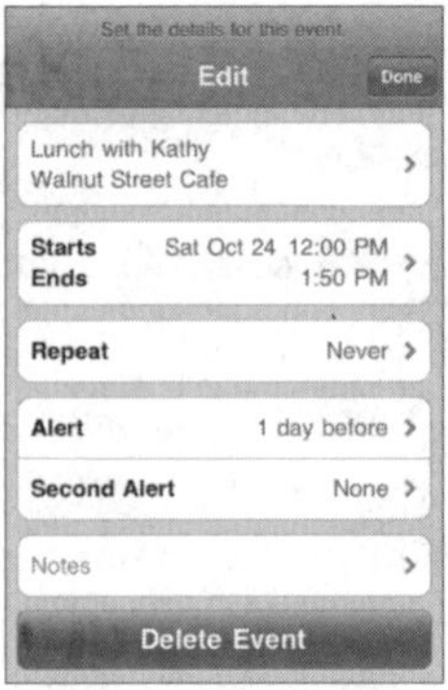

Figure 5.22
Editing an event.

Creating events

Creating events on the iPod is simple. Just tap the plus icon in the top-right corner of the screen to produce the Add Event screen, where you'll find fields for Title & Location, Start & End, Repeat, Alert, Calendar, and Notes. In more detail:

Title & Location. The title of the event will appear when you select the event's date in Month view. Both an event's title and location appear in the Day-view list. And in List view, you see just the event's title. As with any other field on the iPod, just type the entries and tap Save when you're done.

Start & End. The title is explanation enough. Just tap the Starts field, and enter a date and time by using the spinning wheels at the bottom of the screen (**Figure 5.23**). Ditto with the Ends field. If the event lasts all day, tap the All-Day On/Off switch.

Figure 5.23
Set the duration of an event.

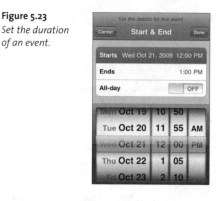

Unlike most calendar applications you're familiar with, this one lets you create events that span multiple days. Just dial in a different day when you tap Ends.

Repeat. You can create an event that occurs every day, week, 2 weeks, month, or year. This method is a convenient way to remind yourself of your kid's weekly piano lesson or your own wedding anniversary.

Alert. A fat lot of good an electronic calendar does you if you're not paying attention to the date or time. Tap Alert and direct the iPod to sound an alert at a specific interval before the event's start time: 5, 15, or 30 minutes; 1 or 2 hours; 1 or 2 days before; or on the date of the event.

You can create two alerts per event—useful when you want to remind yourself of events for the day and need another mental nudge a few minutes before the event occurs. Regrettably, you can't change the alert sound; you can only turn it on or off in the Sound Settings screen.

Calendar. Using this command, you can assign the new event to any calendar you have on your iPod.

Notes. Feel free to type a bit of text to remind yourself exactly why you're allowing Bob Whosis to dominate your Thursday afternoon.

Syncing events

Your computer and your iPod have a nice sharing relationship with regard to events. When you create an event on one device, it's copied to the other, complete with title, location, start and end times, alerts (likely called *alarms* in your computer's calendar program), and notes.

As I explain in Chapter 2, you can pick and choose the computer-based calendars you want to sync with the iPod within iTunes's Info tab. If you have an Exchange or MobileMe account, calendar events associated with those accounts are pushed to your iPod (and the iPod pushes right back those events that you create on it).

Deleting events

Quite frankly, deleting events by using the iPod's interface is a pain in the neck. As I mention earlier in the chapter, you tap an event, tap the Edit button in the Event screen, tap the red Delete Event button at the bottom of the screen, and then tap Delete Event again. This procedure is a very inefficient way to delete events, particularly lots of events that have expired. You're better off letting iTunes lend a hand.

To do so, plug your iPod into your computer and then select it in iTunes' Source list. Click the Info tab, and configure the Calendars delete option to read *Do Not Sync Events Older Than X Days,* where *X* is the number of past days you're willing to keep expired events on your iPod. When you next sync your iPod, events that occurred more than *X* days before the current date will be removed from the iPod (**Figure 5.24**).

Figure 5.24
It's easier to delete lots of events through iTunes.

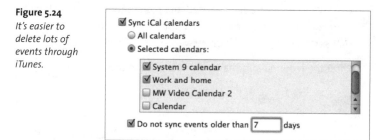

If you'd like to delete multiple future events, delete them from your computer's calendar. If you're using a nonpush account, when you sync your iPod, the events will disappear from the iPod's calendar as well. When Exchange and your MobileMe account are set up to synchronize calendars, deleting events either on the server or on the iPod will cause the event to vanish from every synced service and device.

Subscribing to a calendar

You can also subscribe to Web-based calendars with your iPod, which supports both CalDAV and iCal formats. To do so, follow these steps:

1. Travel to Settings > Mail, Contacts, Calendars, and tap Add Account.

2. Tap Other in the Add Account screen.

3. In the Calendars area of the Other screen, choose either Add CalDAV Account or Add Subscribed Calendar.

   Which you choose depends on the kind of calendar you want to subscribe to. iCal calendars are generally available to the public and require only that you have a server address in the form *example.com/example.ics*. iCalShare (http://icalshare.com) is a repository for such public calendars.

   CalDAV calendars are server-based and require that you know the name of the host server and have a user name and password for that server.

4. Enter the required information to subscribe to the calendar.

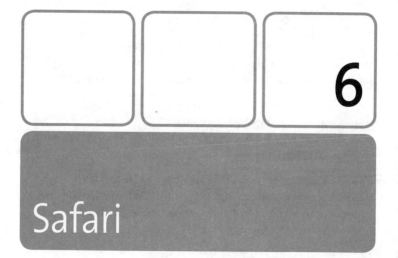

6

Safari

From Day One, the iPod touch has had a real live Web browser, very much like the one on your computer. In this chapter, I show you how to use it to best advantage. Let's go surfing!

Importing Bookmarks

I know you're eager to start surfing the Web with Safari, but you'll find the experience far more pleasant if you first sync your Safari (Mac) or Safari or Internet Explorer (Windows) bookmarks to your iPod. This is easy to do:

1. Jack your iPod touch into your computer's USB 2.0 port, launch iTunes (if it doesn't launch automatically), select the iPod in iTunes' Source list, and click the Info tab.

2. In the Web Browser area of the window, on a Mac, enable the Sync Safari Bookmarks option (**Figure 6.1**); on a Windows PC, enable the Sync Bookmarks From option and choose either Safari or Internet Explorer from the pop-up menu.

Figure 6.1
Syncing Safari within the Mac version of iTunes.

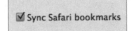

3. Export your bookmarks, if you're not using Safari or Internet Explorer.

   To sync your bookmarks with the iPod via iTunes, you must make sure that your bookmarks are in one of these two browsers. If you're using a browser such as Mozilla Firefox, check its help system for details on exporting its bookmarks.

4. Open Safari and choose File > Import Bookmarks, or fire up Internet Explorer and choose File > Import and Export.

5. Navigate to the bookmarks file you saved.

   Your bookmarks are now in a browser that's compatible with the iPod. When you next sync your iPod, those bookmarks will be available to the iPod's copy of Safari.

Surfin' Safari

When you first tap the Safari icon at the bottom of the iPod's Home screen, you may be surprised to see a full (though tiny) representation of a Web page appear before your eyes. Safari on the iPod touch is nearly the real deal. (In "Seeing Safari's limits" later in this chapter, I talk about how that isn't quite the case.)

At first glance, though, it's the real *small* deal. The pages Safari displays on the iPod are Lilliputian at first, but you have ways to make these pages legible:

■ **Turn the iPod on its side.** Yes, Safari, like nearly all the included apps, works in both portrait and landscape orientation. It displays the entire width of a Web page in either view, so when you switch to landscape orientation, you see more detail as the page enlarges to fill the iPod's screen (**Figure 6.2**).

Figure 6.2

A Web page in landscape orientation, showing Safari's tool icons.

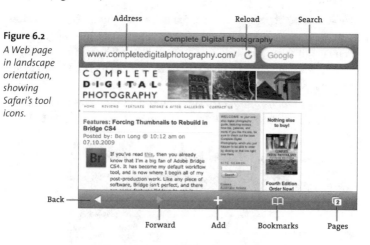

Address   Reload   Search

Back   Forward   Add   Bookmarks   Pages

- **Stretch the page open.** You can enlarge the page by using the stretch gesture (see Chapter 1). When the page is enlarged, tap and drag to reposition it.

- **Double-tap a column.** Most Web pages include columns of text and graphics. To zoom in on a single column, double-tap it. That column expands to fill the iPod's screen. To shrink the page to its original size, double-tap the screen again.

- **Double-tap part of the page.** If a Web page lacks columns, you can still zoom in by double-tapping the page.

Browsing the Web

Like any good browser, Safari provides numerous ways to get around the Web. Let me count the ways.

Getting addressed

Like your computer's Web browser, Safari has an Address field at the top of its main window. (If you don't see the Address field, just tap the gray menu bar at the top of the screen, and you'll be taken to the top of the page, where the Address field is revealed.) To travel to a Web site, tap in this field. When you do, the iPod's keyboard appears. If ever there were an argument for using Safari in landscape orientation, this feature is it, because the iPod's keyboard is far less cramped this way (**Figure 6.3**).

Figure 6.3
The landscape Safari keyboard (with the .com key held down).

Type the Web address you want to visit. The iPod and its keyboard make this process as easy for you as possible. To begin with, you needn't type **http://www**. Safari understands that just about every Web address begins this way and doesn't require you to type the prefix. Just type **examplesite**; then tap the .com key at the bottom of the keyboard (even .com is unnecessary sometimes), and tap Go. In a short time, the page you desire will appear.

> **tip** If a site's URL ends with something like .net or .org, you needn't key that in. Just tap and hold the keyboard's .com entry until a pop-up menu appears, offering additional .net, .edu, and .org entries. Glide your finger over to the entry you want, and let go. The address will complete with the extension you chose.

Safari offers some other convenient shortcuts for entering addresses. If you've visited the site before, for example, it's likely to be in Safari's History list. If so, just begin typing the address, and it will appear below the Address field (**Figure 6.4**). Tap the address to go to that Web site.

Figure 6.4
The iPod's History list can save typing.

> **tip** If the Address field is full when you tap it, you can erase its contents quickly by tapping the X icon that appears at the right edge of the field.

note If you're concerned that the contents of your iPod's History list may give others pause, you can clear the list. See "Setting Safari" at the end of the chapter to learn how.

If you need to type a more complex address—**example.com/pictures/vacation.html**, for example—the iPod's default keyboard for Safari can help, because it includes both period (.) and slash (/) keys.

To leave the keyboard behind without doing anything, tap the Cancel button. If the page you're trying to visit is taking too long to load, or if you've changed your mind about visiting it, just tap the X that appears next to the Address field while the page is loading. Safari will stop loading the page. If you'd like to reload a page that's fully loaded, tap the Reload icon next to the Address field (the one that takes the place of the X when a page is completely loaded).

Searching

You can also conduct Google or Yahoo searches from the keyboard. To begin a search, just tap the magnifying-glass icon in the top-left corner of a Safari window. This tap causes the keyboard to appear and the insertion point to blink in the Search field. Enter your query in this field and then tap Google or Yahoo (depending on which search engine you're using).

By default, the iPod uses Google search. To switch to Yahoo, go to the Settings screen, and tap Safari. Tap Search Engine and then tap Yahoo.

Navigating with links

Links work just as they do in your computer's browser. Just tap a link to go to the associated Web page. Two things are worth noting:

- Safari is sometimes reluctant to use a link while it's still loading a Web page. To speed things up, tap the X icon next to the Address field to stop the current page from loading; then tap the link to load its target immediately. (In some cases, you'll see a blank page instead of the page you were on, because Safari had started to load the new page but hadn't completed the process. In such cases, tap the back-arrow icon to return to the previous page.)

- When you hover your mouse pointer over a link in your computer's Web browser, you can view information about where that link will take you. The iPod offers a more powerful, though hidden, capability. Just tap and hold a link, and a sheet scrolls up from the bottom. This sheet displays not only the full address of the link, but also four options—Open, Open in New Page, Copy, and Cancel—whose names match their purposes (**Figure 6.5**).

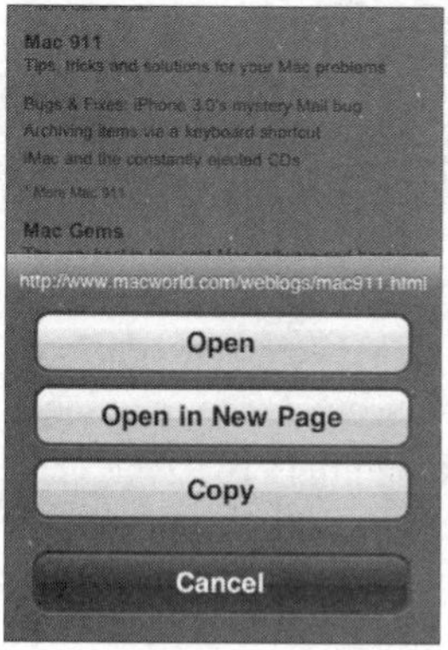

Figure 6.5
Tap and hold a link to see these options.

Going back and forward

Just like your computer's Web browser, Safari has Back and Forward arrows for moving through sites you've visited.

Saving pages

In the bottom-right corner of the Safari screen, you'll see a small Pages icon. Tap it, and you'll see a small representation of the page you're currently viewing. Tap the New Page button in the bottom-left corner of the screen, and you can create a new empty Web page, saving the page you were just viewing in the process (**Figure 6.6**). This feature is the iPod's equivalent of browser tabs.

Figure 6.6
Safari lets you save up to eight pages.

You can repeat this process to save as many as eight pages; the Pages icon displays the number of pages you've stored. To visit one of your saved pages, tap the Pages icon, and swipe your finger across the display to move back or forward through the saved pages. To view a page full-screen, tap its thumbnail or tap the Done button while its thumbnail is on view. To delete a page, tap the red X in the top-left corner of the page.

note The contents of saved pages aren't cached to the iPod—just their locations—so you won't be able to read them if your iPod is offline (when you can't access a Wi-Fi network).

Navigating with bookmarks

You heeded my advice to import your computer browser's bookmarks, right? Great. Bookmarks are another fine way to get where you want to go.

Just tap the Bookmarks icon at the bottom of Safari's screen. The Bookmarks screen will appear, replete with your bookmarks organized as they were on your computer. By this, I mean that if you've organized your computer's bookmarks in folders, that's just how they'll appear on your iPod. Bookmarks that you've placed in Safari's Bookmarks bar are contained in their own folder, named (aptly enough) Bookmarks Bar.

Tap a folder to view the bookmarks it contains. To travel to a bookmark's target page, tap the bookmark.

Working with bookmarks

Bookmarks are important-enough components of Safari that they deserve more than this so-far-brief mention. How, for example, do you create bookmarks, organize and edit the ones you have, and delete those you no longer need? Like this.

Creating bookmarks

You've found a Web site you like while surfing with the iPod. To book-mark the site, follow these steps:

1. Tap the plus (+) icon at the bottom of the screen.

   In the sheet that appears, the first option is Add Bookmark. (I look at the other two options soon.)

2. Tap Add Bookmark.

   The Add Bookmark screen opens, displaying the name of the book-mark. If the name is too long for your liking, edit it with the iPod's standard text-editing keyboard.

3. Tap the Bookmarks entry, and choose a location for your bookmark.

   When you do this, a list that contains your bookmarks-folder hierarchy appears. Tap the folder where you'd like to file your bookmark. From now on, this folder is where you'll find that bookmark (**Figure 6.7**).

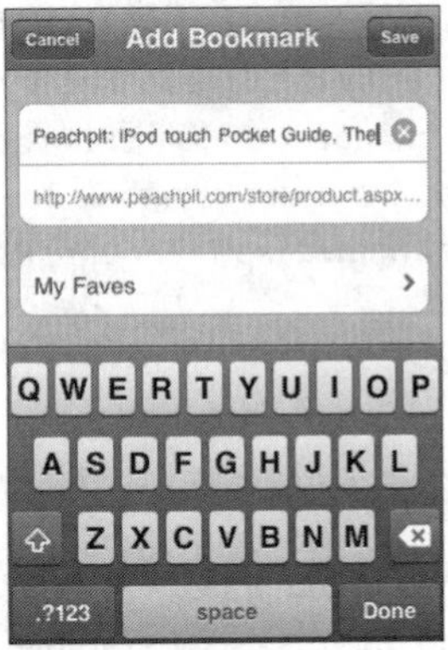

Figure 6.7
Creating a bookmark.

4. Tap Save to save the bookmark in this location, or tap Cancel to cancel the bookmarking operation.

Organizing and editing bookmarks

If you're as organized as I am (meaning not very), your bookmarks may be a bit of a mess. Although you're better off organizing the bookmarks on your computer and then syncing them to your iPod, you can organize them on the iPod as well. To do so, follow along:

1. Tap the Bookmarks icon.

2. In the resulting Bookmarks screen, tap the Edit button.

3. To delete an item, tap the red minus (–) icon that appears next to it.

The red minus icon appears next to all entries in the screen save History, Bookmarks Bar, and Bookmarks Menu—in short, all the items you've created but none of the items that the iPod requires.

You'll also notice the three-line reposition icon to the right of these marked items, indicating that you can change their positions in the list by dragging the icons up or down. You can also rename your bookmark, change its URL, or file it in a different folder by tapping its name while in editing mode and then making those changes in the resulting Edit Bookmark screen.

Additionally, you can create a new folder this way:

1. Tap the New Folder icon in the bottom-right section of the screen to open an Edit Folder screen.

2. Use the onscreen keyboard to give your folder a name; then choose a location for it by tapping the field below, which displays the name of the folder you're currently in (such as Bookmarks Bar).

3. Tap this field, and up pops the bookmarks hierarchy.

4. Tap the folder in which you'd like to place this new folder.

5. Tap the arrow icon in the top-left section of the screen.

   Your folder is created.

Getting more from the plus icon

As I mention in "Creating bookmarks" earlier in this chapter, when you tap the plus (+) icon at the bottom of Safari's screen, you see two options after Add Bookmark: Add to Home Screen and Mail Link to This Page. (OK, you see a Cancel button too, so technically, there are *four* options.) These two buttons work this way:

Add to Home Screen. When you tap this button, an Add to Home screen appears, displaying the name of the Web page you're currently viewing with some kind of icon next to the page's name (**Figure 6.8**). (Some Web sites have gone to the trouble to create a cool icon that looks great on an iPod touch and iPhone. Other icons are just undistinguished thumbnails of a portion of the page.) You're welcome to rename the saved page by using the keyboard.

Figure 6.8

Adding a Web site to your Home screen.

Click Add, and an icon representing that Web page is created in the iPod's Home screen (**Figure 6.9**). In the future, when you tap that icon, Safari will launch and take you directly to that page.

Figure 6.9

The icon of a Web site on the Home screen.

tip Should you grow tired of this icon, you can remove it just as you can remove other expendable items (meaning applications other than the ones originally included with the iPod) from the iPod's Home screen. Tap and hold the icon until all the icons start wiggling. Then tap the X in the top-left corner of the icon you want to delete, and it's gone.

Mail Link to This Page. If you find a Web page that cries out to be shared with your nearest as well as dearest, tap Mail Link to This Page. When you do, a new, unaddressed mail message opens. The Subject heading is the name of the Web page, and the body of the message contains a link to the page. All you need to do is address the message and tap Send.

Understanding Safari and RSS

Safari supports RSS (Really Simple Syndication), the standard for distributing Web headlines. To view collections of these headlines (called *feeds*) on your iPod, just locate a page's RSS link and tap it. The page that appears bears a blue bar at the top, along with the name of the site connected to the feed—Mac 911, for example (**Figure 6.10**). The site's headlines appear below the blue bar. Tap a headline to read the full story.

Figure 6.10
A Safari RSS feed.

tip RSS URLs are clumsy to enter yourself; they're long and rarely contain real words. For this reason, bookmarking those that you intend to revisit is a good idea.

Seeing Safari's limits

Earlier in this chapter, I hint that although the iPod's version of Safari is about as full-featured as you're likely to find on a mobile iPod, it doesn't have all the capabilities of your computer's browser. The following sections discuss its limitations.

No Flash support

Many modern Web sites greet you with luxurious animations, flickering icons, and animated menus created with Adobe's Web-animation design tool, Flash. The iPod doesn't support Flash, and because it doesn't, you may see nothing at all on such a site's home page. Ideally, the designer took into account the fact that not everyone likes (or, in the case of the iPod touch and iPhone, can use) Flash and inserted a Skip Animation link that takes you to a Flashless version of the site.

Similarly, many of the movies you find on the Web are Flash-based. If, while traipsing through a Web site, you see a small blue box with a question mark inside it, you're looking at the placeholder for a Flash movie. Tapping that icon will do you no good whatsoever.

The good news is that the iPod will play a lot of QuickTime content (though not all). As the iPod touch and iPhone increase in popularity, Web sites likely will increase their use of QuickTime.

No downloading

You're accustomed to downloading files with computers and Web browsers. You give up that feature when using the iPod touch's browser, however, because it's not supported.

No Find

Web pages can be packed with information, and the iPod's screen is a pretty small place to view that much content. I'd love to be able to pull up a Search field and key in a word or phrase I seek. I can't.

Setting Safari

Like other iPod applications, Safari has its own collection of settings. As you might guess, you find them by tapping Settings in the iPod's Home screen and then tapping Safari in the Settings screen (**Figure 6.11**).

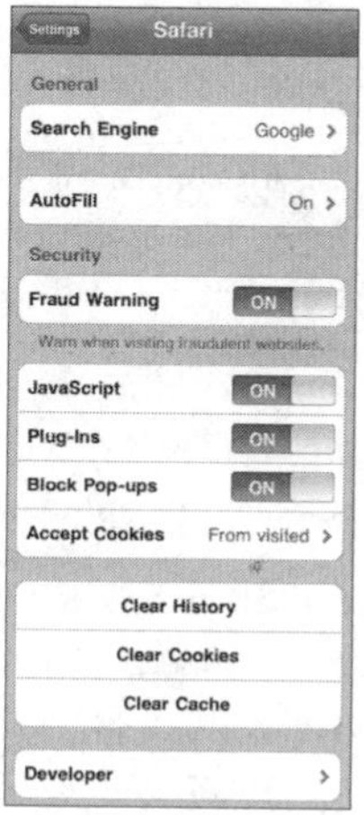

Figure 6.11
Safari settings.

Settings	Safari
General	
Search Engine	Google >
AutoFill	On >
Security	
Fraud Warning	ON
Warn when visiting fraudulent websites.	
JavaScript	ON
Plug-Ins	ON
Block Pop-ups	ON
Accept Cookies	From visited >
Clear History	
Clear Cookies	
Clear Cache	
Developer	>

These settings include the following:

Search Engine. The iPod can use either Google or Yahoo for its Web searches. Choose the one you want here.

AutoFill. This feature was new with the 3.0 software. AutoFill, like your computer's Web browser, can fill in contact information, user names, and passwords. To enable those options, tap AutoFill and toggle the Use Contact Info and Names & Passwords sliders to On.

Fraud Warning. Your iPod will warn you when it believes you're about to enter a Web site that pretends to be something it's not. This might be a Web site that pretends to belong to your bank or credit card company but exists only to steal money from people who unwarily provide their account information.

JavaScript. JavaScript is a scripting language that helps make Web sites more interactive. By default, Safari allows JavaScript to work. If you care to disable JavaScript for some reason, you do it with this On/Off switch.

Plug-Ins. The iPod supports some plug-ins that allow it to display or play certain Web content—QuickTime movies and audio, for example. You can turn off these plug-ins by toggling this switch to Off.

Block Pop-Ups. I make a lot of my living by writing for advertising-based Web sites, but I've yet to see a pop-up window that did more than annoy me. If you're haunted by pop-up ads, leave this option's switch set to On.

Accept Cookies. Many Web sites leave little markers called *cookies* stored in your Web browser. Cookies can store information such as when you visited the site and which pages you saw there. Sometimes, they also store information such as your user name and password for that site.

The Accept Cookies setting gives you a measure of control:

- You can choose never to accept them (which some people consider to be more secure and private, but which forces you to reenter passwords and user names each time you return).

- You can opt to accept just those cookies sent by each site you visit. (Some sites plant cookies from their advertisers, and this option prevents that behavior.)

- You can choose to always accept cookies, which means that your iPod is now a cookie-gathering machine. The default setting is From Visited, which I think nicely balances privacy and convenience.

Clear History, Clear Cookies, and Clear Cache. This group of three buttons in the Safari Settings screen allows you to wipe your tracks:

- Earlier, I told you that when you start typing a URL in Safari's Address field, the iPod makes suggestions based on past searches. To stop this behavior, tap Clear History.

- If you're concerned that the iPod's stored cookies reveal more about your browsing habits than you're comfortable with, tap Clear Cookies.

- Safari's cache stores some of the contents of pages you visit so that they open faster when you revisit. If new content isn't showing up, and you believe that it should, tapping Clear Cache will help by forcing Safari to reload entire pages that were previously cached.

When you tap any of these buttons, you're asked to confirm that you really want to perform the action.

Developer. You can turn on a Debug Console within Safari if you're interested in seeing any coding errors a Web page might have. If you're an übergeek and find such errors fascinating, knock yourself out and switch it on. Everyone else, feel free to leave it off.

7

Photos and YouTube

Your iPod touch is an audio wonder, but it also offers its share of visual delights. Although it lacks the 5G iPod nano's and iPhone's camera, it's capable of displaying pictures that you sync to the iPod, as well as those that you receive via email and copy from Safari. Also on the visual front, your iPod touch can play YouTube videos in a separate YouTube application—no Web browser required. In this chapter, I scrutinize both talents in detail.

You Ought to Be in Pictures

Tapping Photos in the iPod's Home screen is the digital equivalent of flipping open your wallet to reveal a seemingly endless stream of pictures of the kids, the dog, and that recent trip to Coober Pedy. The iPod's Photos application, however, is no mere repository for pictures. Flick a finger, and you're flying from photo to photo. Spread your fingers, and you've zoomed in on a picture's most poignant portion. If you have a more formal presentation in mind—a showing of your child's first birthday party for Grandma and Grandpa, for example—you can create something far grander in the form of a slideshow. And if you have movies in your Mac's iPhoto library, the Photos application can play those too. To learn about these and other visual wonders, just follow along.

The face of Photos

When you tap Photos, you see the Photo Albums screen, which acts as the gateway to the images stored on your camera (**Figure 7.1**). In this screen, you'll find at least one entry, and there'll be more after you sync photos to your iPod.

Figure 7.1
The Photo Albums screen.

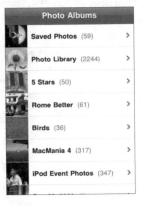

Photo Albums	
Saved Photos (59)	>
Photo Library (2244)	>
5 Stars (50)	>
Rome Better (61)	>
Birds (36)	>
MacMania 4 (317)	>
iPod Event Photos (347)	>

The first entry is Saved Photos. Tap it to see the images you've captured by using the iPod's screen-capture shortcut (hold the Home button while quickly pressing the Sleep/Wake button), the images that have been sent to you in email, and the images you've copied from Safari.

To the left of this entry in the Photo Albums screen, you'll see a thumbnail image of the last picture added to the album. To the right of the entry, in parentheses, you'll see the combined number of images that this album contains—*Saved Photos (17)*, for example. The > character at the far-right edge of the screen indicates that when you tap this entry, you'll be taken to another screen. That other screen, called Saved Photos, contains thumbnail images of all the photos in this album.

The next entry, Photo Library, contains all the photos on your iPod save for those in the Saved Photos library. It too bears a thumbnail (not one of your images, but a sunflower), and it displays the total number of images in the library—*Photo Library (2239)*, for example. Tap this entry, and in the resulting Photo Library screen, you'll see thumbnail images of all the photos on your iPod (again, excluding the Saved Photos images).

As you learned in Chapter 2, you can sync photo albums created by such programs as iPhoto, Aperture, Photoshop Elements, and Photoshop Albums. When you do, these albums appear in the Photo Albums screen as separate entries, each featuring a thumbnail of the first image in the album as well as the number of images in the album—*Father's Day (48)* or *Family Holiday (92)*, for example.

When you select your Pictures folder (Mac, Windows Vista, and Windows 7), My Pictures (Windows XP), or a folder of your choosing within iTunes' Photos tab, any folders contained within those folders are presented as separate albums. So, for example, if your Pictures folder holds three folders that contain pictures—say, *Betty's Birthday*, *Dog Polisher*, and *Cheeses Loved and Lost*—each of those items appears as a separate album in the Photo Albums screen. Again, each album lists the number of images it contains in parentheses.

If you're a Mac user and store your pictures in iPhoto '09, you're probably aware that iPhoto automatically groups pictures taken during the same general period—a single day, for example. In the Photos tab within iTunes, you can ask that iPhoto's 1, 3, 5, 10, or 20 most recent events be synced to your iPod (**Figure 7.2**). Additionally, with iTunes 9, you can sync Faces albums to your iPod touch (as I explain in Chapter 2).

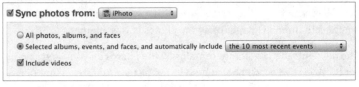

Figure 7.2 *Sync iPhoto's most recent events to your iPod.*

iPhoto users have one additional advantage: When you connect a 5G iPod nano, an iPhone 3GS, or one of today's pocket camcorders (such as Pure Digital's popular Flip camcorders), iPhoto will offer to import that device's video. I'll explain the mechanics of this process shortly.

Picture and movie viewing

As I mention earlier in this chapter, when you're in an album's screen, you see all the pictures in that album arrayed four across as thumbnail images (**Figure 7.3**). You can see 20 complete thumbnails onscreen. If your album contains more than 20 images, just flick your finger up across the display to scroll more images into view. To see a picture or movie full-screen, just tap it.

From this thumbnails screen, you can also copy pictures and movies. To do that, just tap and hold the picture or movie you want to copy. A Copy bubble will appear. Tap it, and the item is copied to the iPod's clipboard.

Figure 7.3
*A photo album's
thumbnail
images.*

From this thumbnails screen, you can also copy pictures and movies. To do that, just tap and hold the picture or movie you want to copy. A Copy bubble will appear. Tap it, and the item is copied to the iPod's clipboard.

Currently, the iPod's Mail application is the only Apple application that lets you paste images and movies.

note If you attempt to paste images or movies into a note that you create in the Notes application, you paste only the names of the items, not the images or movies themselves.

Setting Album thumbnail-screen options

You know that when you tap the name of an album, that album appears with its contents displayed as thumbnails. At the bottom of the album screen are two buttons: Options (represented by an arrow rising out of a picture frame) and Play.

The Play button. Tapping this button, regardless of the kind of album you've selected, starts a slideshow of the pictures in that library. You can view slideshows in either horizontal or vertical orientation.

The timing and transitions of a slideshow are determined by options set for the Photos entry in the iPod's Settings screen. You have the option to play each slide for 2, 3, 5, 10, or 20 seconds, and you can choose among Cube, Dissolve, Ripple, Wipe Across, and Wipe Down transitions.

When you tap the screen during a slideshow, transparent gray bars appear briefly at the top and bottom of the screen. The top one displays a left-pointing arrow bearing the name of the currently selected photo album. As with most iPod screens, you tap this arrow to move up one screen in the iPod's hierarchy. You'll also see an entry such as *8 of 48*, which tells you which one of the total number of pictures you're looking at. The bottom bar includes an Options button, along with Previous and Next buttons. (I describe these buttons in "Working with the picture screen" later in this chapter.)

The Options button. When you tap this button while viewing the thumbnail images of the Saved Photos screen, you'll see three buttons at the bottom of the screen: Share, Copy, and Delete. They work this way:

■ **Share.** Tap one or more images and then tap Share, and two or three buttons scroll up from the bottom of the screen. The first, Email, does what you'd expect. The selected images are imported into an empty email message. Just fill in the recipient and add a Subject line, and you're ready to send.

If you have a MobileMe account configured on your iPod, and you've selected a single image or movie, a Send to MobileMe button will also be present. Tap it, and a MobileMe screen appears. Within this screen, you assign a title to your image or movie and, optionally, add a description. Next, select one of the MobileMe Galleries you've published. (You must have published such a gallery for this option to work.) Finally, then tap the Publish button. The image or movie will be uploaded to the selected MobileMe Gallery.

- **Copy.** Tap this option, and the selected images and/or movies are copied to the iPod's clipboard. Then you can paste them into compatible applications (refer to "Picture and movie viewing" earlier in this chapter).

- **Delete.** Select images and/or movies and tap Delete, and they're removed.

When you're viewing any album's thumbnail page *other* than Saved Photos, you'll find just the Share and Copy buttons. They perform exactly the same way as the options I've just described.

Setting picture-screen options

When you tap a thumbnail image, you'll see that image and, briefly, a gray bar along the bottom that contains three buttons: Options, Back, and Next. Back and Next are obvious, but Options presents a couple of choices that aren't available in an album's thumbnails screen.

When you tap the Options button, the bottom of the screen rolls up to display four or five buttons—Email Photo, Send to MobileMe (this is the "or five" button; it won't appear if you don't have a MobileMe account on your iPod), Assign to Contact, Use As Wallpaper, and Cancel (**Figure 7.4**).

Figure 7.4
Options available in the picture screen.

You know what Email Photo and Send to MobileMe do. As for the other two:

- **Assign to Contact.** You recall from Chapter 5 that you can assign pictures to the names in the Contacts application. This button is one other avenue for doing that.

- **Use As Wallpaper.** When your iPod's screen goes black, it hasn't turned itself off. Rather, it's locked itself and switched off the screen to save power. When you click the Home button to bring the screen back to life, you see the Locked screen. The background image for this screen is the iPod's wallpaper. If you'd like that wallpaper to be the currently displayed image, tap this button.

Orienteering

For those of you keeping score at home, Photos is one of those areas of the iPod that has always worked in both portrait and landscape orientation. When viewing pictures and movies, it's best to view them in the orientation in which they were originally shot. So, for example, if you shot a picture holding a camera the "normal" way, you'd turn the iPod on its side to view the picture in landscape orientation (**Figure 7.5**). If you turned the camera 90 degrees to take another picture, hold the iPod in its normal orientation to look at that image in portrait view.

Figure 7.5
Widescreen picture view.

The same goes for videos that you've synced from iPhoto. Hold the iPod normally, and you'll see black bars above and below the video. Turn the iPod on its side, and the video should fill the screen.

Working with the picture screen

In addition to letting you rotate your pictures by flipping your iPod around, the screen in which you view individual images offers some cool features. When viewing a picture in Saved Photos, an album, or the Photo Albums screen, you'll briefly see a transparent gray control bar at the bottom of the screen, displaying three symbols: Options, Previous, and Next (**Figure 7.6**). This control bar conveniently disappears after a couple of seconds so that you can see the complete picture without obstruction. To bring it back, just tap the display.

Figure 7.6
Control-bar options in the picture screen.

Options ——

Previous   Next

When you view a picture in the Saved Photos album, you see one additional icon: Trash. If you've synced or captured an image with the iPod's screen-shot button combination and now regret that action, just tap the Trash icon, and in the sheet that appears, tap the red Delete Photo icon.

The left- and right-arrow icons that represent the Previous and Next commands do just what they suggest. Tap the left arrow, and you go back to the previous image in the album. Tap the right arrow, and you're on to the next image. If you tap and hold these icons, you zip through your pictures at increasing speed.

Viewing pictures

Tapping those Previous and Next icons is the less impressive way to move from picture to picture. For a far more stirring demonstration of the iPod's slickness, swipe your finger to the left to advance to the next picture or to the right to retreat one picture. You're guaranteed to get an "Oooh!" from the audience on this one.

While you've got your audience in the "Oooh"ing mood, try this: Double-tap an interesting spot in a picture. Like magic, the screen zooms and places that spot as close to the center of the screen as it can. Drag your finger on the picture to reposition it. If you'd like greater control of how large the image is, use the spread gesture (which I discuss in Chapter 1) to make it grow incrementally. Regrettably, the iPod won't remember how you've repositioned and resized the picture. Also regrettably, you can't swipe to the next picture until you've restored the picture to its original size. You can do this by double-tapping the display again or by pinching the image down to its native size.

Swiping is good at any time, even during a slideshow. If, while viewing a slideshow, you'd like to take control, just tap the display to stop the slideshow, or swipe your finger to the left to advance or right to go back. When you manually navigate to the photo that precedes or follows the one on view, the slideshow is canceled. To restart it, you must return to the album screen and tap the Play button, which starts the show from the first image.

These settings are the defaults. If you've configured the Photos settings so that the Repeat and Shuffle options are on, the slideshow will behave a bit differently. To begin with, the show will reach the end and then start over, continuing to play until you tell it to stop by tapping the display. And if Shuffle is on, the photos in the selected album will play in random order.

Viewing movies

When you tap a movie that you've synced to the iPod, you see a different interface from what you're accustomed to seeing for pictures. At the bottom of this screen are three buttons: Back, Play, and Next. To move to the previous movie in the album (if there is one), tap Back. To travel to the subsequent movie, tap Next. And to play the movie, tap either the Play button at the bottom of the screen or the larger Play button in the middle of the screen. (When you tap either button, the Play button at the bottom of the screen changes to a Pause button.)

Along the top of the screen is a series of thumbnail images (**Figure 7.7** on the following page), which is the movie timeline. On this timeline is a narrow silver playhead. To navigate quickly through the movie— forward or backward—just drag the playhead. You can get much finer control by tapping and holding the playhead. When you do, the time-line expands to show a subset of the thumbnail images closest to the playhead.

note   In the thumbnails screen of an album that holds nothing but movies, you'll see an Options button, just as you'd see this button on any other thumbnails screen. Tap it, however, and you see a screen that reads No Photos or Videos. Weird.

Figure 7.7
Viewing a movie in the Photos application.

YouTube

YouTube remains the Big Cheese for watching politicians kill their careers with a few ill-chosen words, frat boys set themselves on fire, and felines impersonate Elvis. Because YouTube is so popular, it only makes sense that the iPod offers you a way to watch its content. It does via the YouTube application.

Navigating YouTube

Tap the YouTube icon in the iPod's Home screen, and you'll see a screen that resembles the one you view when you enter the iPod's Music area. Like the Music screen, this one has five icons along the bottom. By default, these icons are Featured, Most Viewed, Search, Favorites, and the ever-popular More (**Figure 7.8**).

Figure 7.8
Icons in the YouTube screen.

Here's what you'll find when you tap each icon.

Featured

Tap Featured, and you get a list of YouTube videos that the service believes most worthy of your attention (**Figure 7.9**). To play one, just tap it. The video will stream to your iPod via a Wi-Fi connection. (If your iPod isn't connected to a Wi-Fi network, of course, you'll see nothing at all.) When you scroll to the bottom of the list, you'll see a Load More entry. Tap it, and more videos are added to the list.

Figure 7.9
Featured YouTube videos.

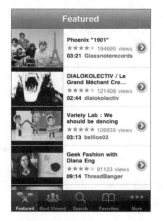

If a video's title, such as *Simon's Cat 'Let Me In!'*, doesn't provide you enough information, feel free to tap the blue icon to the right of the video's title. When you do, you'll see the name of the movie you selected at the top of the screen and three buttons below: Add to Favorites, Add to Playlist, and Share Video.

Tap Add to Favorites, and that video is added to your list of favorites, making it easy to find it again. (I reveal more about favorites shortly.)

You can create playlists of YouTube videos via an option in the More screen. When you tap Add to Playlists, you can choose a playlist to add a video to. Alternatively, tap the plus (+) button in the Add to Playlist screen, and create a playlist right then and there.

When you tap Share Video, a new email message opens. The Subject line includes the title of the video, and the message body contains *Check out this video on YouTube:*, followed by a link to the video. (You can edit *Check out this video on YouTube:* to anything you like.) When you complete the To field and tap Send, the email message is sent via your default email account (as configured in Mail Settings).

The description screen also includes a Related Videos area. If YouTube has videos that it believes are similar in theme to the one you've chosen, it lists them here.

Tap yet another blue icon to the right of the movie in this screen, and you arrive at the movie's More Info screen. This screen includes a description of the video, the date when the video was added; its category (Drama or Documentary, for example); and its tags, which include anything that the poster thought appropriate, such as *poodle*, *waterslide*, and *ointment;* a Rate, Comment or Flag button for doing just that; and user comments below. To read more comments, tap the Load More comments button at the bottom of the screen.

If you're interested in seeing other videos uploaded by the producer of the video you're currently exploring, tap the More Videos button at the top of the More Info screen (**Figure 7.10**).

Figure 7.10
A YouTube More Videos screen.

Most Viewed

The Most Viewed icon provides you the opportunity to view YouTube's most popular videos—all videos, or the most viewed today or this week. Like the Featured screen, this one carries a Load More entry at the bottom of the list. To watch all, today's most viewed, or this week's most viewed videos, tap the appropriate icon at the top of the screen.

Search

You can search YouTube's catalog of videos, of course, and this button is the way to go about it. Tap Search, and you get a Search field in return. Tap this field, and up pops the iPod's keyboard. Type a search term—*skateboard* or *Mentos,* for example—and YouTube searches for videos that match your query. Then it presents a list of 25 videos that it feels match what you're after. If more than 25 videos are available that match your query, your friend the Load More entry appears at the bottom of the list.

Favorites

As the name hints, here's where you store links to your favorite YouTube videos. To begin streaming one of these videos, just tap its name. To remove a favorite, tap the Edit icon at the top of the screen, tap the red minus (–) icon that appears next to the entry, and then tap Delete (**Figure 7.11**). When you're finished removing favorites, tap Done to return to the Favorites screen.

Figure 7.11
YouTube favorites.

> **tip** When you sign into your YouTube account and add a favorite, that favorite appears not only on your iPod, but also within YouTube in your computer's Web browser.

More

You've read Chapter 3, right? Then this More icon should be no mystery to you. Tap it, and you get additional choices: Most Recent, Top Rated, History, My Videos, Subscriptions, and Playlists.

Most Recent offers a glimpse of the 25 videos most recently added by YouTube, and Top Rated displays YouTube's 25 highest-rated videos.

History details all the videos you've chosen. Yes, *chosen.* You don't have to watch these videos for them to appear in your History list. Just choose them, and even if you cancel playback before they appear, they'll be part of your iPod's YouTube History. If this list is too long, or if you're embarrassed by some of the things you've chosen, tap the red Clear icon at the top of the screen. All History entries disappear.

> **note** The Clear icon is an all-or-nothing affair. Currently, the iPod touch doesn't provide an option to delete individual videos from the History screen.

My Videos lists all the videos you've uploaded to YouTube under your account.

Subscriptions presents a list of the producers or channels you've subscribed to. The number of videos available in a subscription appears next to its name—*Macworld (171)*, for example.

Finally, as I mention earlier, you can create playlists of YouTube videos. To create a playlist, just tap the plus (+) button in the top-left corner of the screen. An Add Playlist screen scrolls up from the bottom. Use the keyboard to name your playlist, and tap the Add button when you're done. You can remove playlists later by tapping the Edit button in the Playlists screen and using the tap-minus-and-then-Delete technique.

Playing YouTube videos

To play a YouTube video, tap it, and the video will begin loading in landscape orientation. You'll see the now-familiar video play controls—Back, Play, and Next—along with a volume slider, timeline, and Scale icon. Like the play controls in the iPod's iPod area, these controls fade a few seconds after they first appear. To force them to reappear, just tap the iPod's display.

In addition to the play controls, you'll see a Favorite icon to the left of the play controls and a Share icon to the right (**Figure 7.12**). Tap Favorite, and the currently playing video is added to your YouTube favorites. Tap Share, and you create another one of those special YouTube recommendation emails that I describe in the "Featured" section earlier in this chapter.

Figure 7.12 *The YouTube play screen.*

The video begins playing when the iPod determines that it has downloaded enough data for the video to play from beginning to end without pausing to download more. When the video concludes, you'll see its More Info screen.

8

The Other Applications

I've covered the iPod touch's major areas: Mail, Safari, Music, Videos, Photos, Calendar, YouTube, the iTunes Store, and the App Store. It's time to turn to the smaller applications, which by default occupy the bulk of the iPod's Home screen: Stocks, Maps, Weather, Voice Memos, Notes, Clock, and Calculator.

If you've used Mac OS X, many of these applications are familiar to you, as most of them are offered in that operating system as *widgets*—small applications that perform limited tasks. On the iPod touch, they're considered to be full-blown applications, even though they're largely single-purpose programs. They work this way.

Stocks

The Stocks application has a lot in common with the Mac OS X Stocks widget. Like that widget, the application displays your chosen stocks and market indexes (Dow Jones Industrial Average and NASDAQ, for example) in the top part of the screen and performance statistics below. Next to each index or stock ticker symbol, you'll see the almost-current share price (results are delayed by 20 minutes), such as *AAPL 188.05,* followed by the day's gain or loss as represented by a green (gain) or red (loss) icon.

By default, the application represents gains and losses in points—*+3.89,* for example. To see the company's market cap—*168.5B,* for example—tap one of these red or green icons. You can toggle to a percentage view by tapping an icon again. Tap once more to return to point view.

note You must be connected to the Internet via a Wi-Fi connection for the results to appear.

To view statistics for a particular index or stock, just tap its name. A graph at the bottom of the screen charts that index's or stock's performance over 1 day, 1 week, 1 month, 3 months, 6 months, 1 year, or 2 years. To choose a time period, just tap the appropriate icon (such as 1d for 1 day or 6m for 6 months).

If you flip the iPod to landscape orientation, you see this graph enlarged. No, this feature isn't for the benefit of people with poor eyesight. Tap and hold this graph, and an orange line appears that tells you the stock price at the time. (The date appears at the top of the screen.) Tap with two fingers, and the iPod tells you the change in points and percentage between one finger and another. So, for example, you might select Apple's stock in 6-month view, place your left index finger on June 1, 2009, and put your right index finger on October 8, 2009 (**Figure 8.1**). You see that the stock rose 49.2 points, or 35.82 percent.

Figure 8.1
*Stocks
application.*

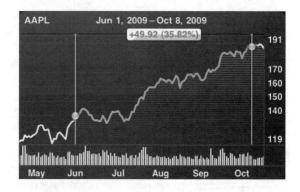

Return the iPod to portrait orientation and swipe a graph to the left, and you'll see news headlines related to the company. (This window scrolls down if there are enough headlines to merit scrolling.) Tap a headline, and Safari launches and displays the story. Swipe once more to the left, and you'll see a table of statistics related to the company, including such things as the day's opening and closing prices and trading volume.

For more detailed information on an index or stock, tap its name to highlight it and then tap the tiny Y! (for Yahoo) icon in the bottom-left corner of the screen. Doing so launches Safari and whisks you to a Yahoo oneSearch page with links related to that item. There, you'll find links to a Yahoo Finance page devoted to the index or stock, with related news, products, full and mobile Web pages, and Web images.

If you tap the *i* (Information) icon in the bottom-right corner of the display, the screen flips to reveal the indexes and stocks that appear on the application's front page. Click the plus (+) icon in the top-left corner and use the iPod's keyboard to add a ticker symbol or company name. In the case of a company name, the iPod will search for matches. If you type **Apple** and tap Search, for example, you'll get a list that includes not only Apple, Inc., but also Nicholas Applegate International and Appleseed

Fund. Tap the search result you want, and it will be added to the bottom of the list. You can reorder the list by dragging an entry up or down in the list by its reorder bar to the right of the entry. To remove items, just tap the red minus (–) icon next to the item's name and then tap the resulting Delete icon.

The Information screen also includes three icons: %, Price, and Mkt Cap. Tap one to determine the default display of gains and losses in the main Stocks screen.

This screen also offers a not-so-obvious icon. To have Safari take you to the Yahoo Finance page, simply tap Yahoo! Finance at the bottom of the screen.

Maps

This application is a version of Google Maps made for the iPod touch and iPhone, and I've found it to be one of the iPod's most useful tools—provided that your iPod is connected to a Wi-Fi network. Without such a network, Maps isn't nearly so useful.

When you *are* connected to a Wi-Fi network, however, you can use Maps to search for interesting locations (including businesses, residences, parks, and landmarks) near where you are or anywhere else in the world. It's the showcase application for the iPod's Location service, which uses Wi-Fi hotspot triangulation technology to pinpoint your iPod's location. You can use it to get driving directions between here and there, and in some cases, you can check traffic conditions along your route.

The Maps application has two major components: Search and Directions. Each is available from the main Maps screen.

Searching and exploring

At the top of the Maps screen, you see a Search field (**Figure 8.2**). Tap it, and up pops the iPod's keyboard. With that keyboard, you can enter any of a variety of search queries, including contacts in your iPod's address book (*Joe Blow*), a business name (*Apple, Inc.*), a town name (*Springfield*), a more-specific town name (*Springfield, MO*), a street or highway name (*Route 66*), a specific street name in a particular town (*Broadway, Springfield, MO*), or a thing (*Beer*).

Figure 8.2
Maps' search feature and the results in the map below.

Tap for Google Street View — Tap for Info window — Dog-ear icon

You can help Maps find its way by entering a more specific search, such as **Main St., Springfield, MO 65802** or **Beer 95521**. In short, the more specific you are in your query, the more accurate Maps will be.

Search views

You can display Maps' search results in four views:

- **Map,** which is a graphical illustration of the area

- **Satellite,** which is a photo captured by an orbiting satellite

- **Hybrid,** which is a satellite view with the names of roads overlaid

- **List,** which is a . . . well, *list* of all the locations pinpointed on the current map

These options are available when you tap the dog-eared-page icon in the bottom-right corner of the iPod's screen (refer to Figure 8.2 in the preceding section). I cover the other options in this screen shortly.

In Map, Satellite, and Hybrid views, search results are denoted by red pushpins that drop onto the map. Tap one of these pins, and the name of the item appears in a description marker. Again, this name can be the name of a contact's address, business, town, or highway.

On the left side of many of these description markers is a round orange icon with a figure of a person inside. Tap this icon, and you see a Google Street View of the location—a series of 360-degree photographs of the area presented in landscape orientation. You can drag your finger around to "look around." To move up or down the street, tap the arrow that over-lays the street (**Figure 8.3**). To return to an overhead view, tap the circle in the bottom-right corner of the map.

Figure 8.3
*Google Street
View.*

The right side of the description marker bears a blue > icon. Tap this icon to go to the location's Info screen.

Info screens

Info screens present any useful information that Maps can obtain about an item, including phone number, email, address, and home-page URL (**Figure 8.4**). The email and URL links are *live*, meaning that when you tap an email address, Mail opens and addresses a message to that contact, and when you tap a URL, Safari opens and displays that Web site.

Figure 8.4
Maps' Info screen.

At the bottom of each Info screen, you'll see five labeled buttons: Directions To Here, Directions From Here, Add to Contacts, Share Location, and Add to Bookmarks. (You may have to scroll the screen to see all these buttons.) They work this way:

- **Directions To Here.** Tap this button to display Maps' Driving Directions interface (which I explain shortly), with the item's address in the End field.

- **Directions From Here.** This feature works similarly. The difference is that the item's address appears in the Driving Directions Start field.

- **Add to Contacts.** This button produces a sheet that bears three buttons: Create New Contact, Add to Existing Contact, and Cancel. Tap the first button, and a New Contact screen appears with the information from the Info screen filled in. You're welcome to add any other information you like, using the standard contact-field tools.

  As for the Add to Existing Contact button, say that your buddy Brabanzio has just started putting in his 8 hours at the local pickle works. You can use Maps to locate said works, tap this icon, and add its information to his contact information.

- **Share Location.** If you've found the perfect sushi joint and want to tell your friends, tap this button. An unaddressed email message pops up. The message's Subject heading includes the name of the location, and the message body contains a link that, when clicked by a recipient, launches a browser and opens Google Maps to that location.

- **Add to Bookmarks.** You can bookmark locations in Maps. Tapping this icon brings up the Add Bookmark screen, where you can rename the bookmark, if you like. When you're done, tap Save, and that location is available from Maps' Bookmarks screen (which, again, I get to shortly).

Bookmarks

The Search field includes a very helpful Bookmarks button. Tap this button to bring up a list of all the locations you've bookmarked, as well as recent search terms and your list of contacts (**Figure 8.5**).

To remove, rename, or reorder select bookmarks, tap the Edit button. In the resulting screen, you can tap the now-expected red minus icon to produce the Delete icon, which you tap to remove the bookmark. You can also tap the bookmark to show the Edit Bookmark screen, where you can edit the bookmark's name. Finally, you can reorder bookmarks by dragging the right side of a bookmark up or down in the list.

Figure 8.5
Maps' Bookmarks screen.

Recents

Tap the Recents button at the bottom of the Bookmarks screen, and you'll see a list of the previous 20 searches done on your iPod. As you conduct a new search, the last search in this list is deleted. These queries are categorized by Search (*pizza*), Start and End (*home to Bob's house*), Location (*Grand Rapids*), and Contact (*Ebenezer Scrooge*). Tap one of these entries, and you see its location—or, in the case of driving directions, locations—on the map.

Contacts

It's swell that your Aunt Vilma sent you a change-of-address card, but where the heck is Fort Dodge, Iowa? Tap the Contacts icon at the bottom of the Bookmarks screen, find Aunt Vilma's name in the long list of contacts, tap her name, and then tap the street address of her new cabin down by the river. Maps will pin her palace in next to no time.

Other dog-ear options

In addition to having access to the Map, Satellite, Hybrid, and List views when you tap the dog-ear icon, you have the two options shown in **Figure 8.6**:

Figure 8.6
The dog-ear screen.

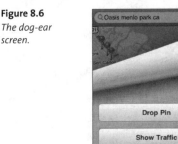

- **Drop Pin.** The first option allows you to drop your own pin on the map. Tap Drop Pin; the dog-ear flips down, and a purple pin appears on the map currently displayed onscreen. Above the pin is a box that tells you to *Drag To Move Pin.* Follow this advice by dragging the pin where you want it. The address of whatever's under the pin will appear in a gray bubble. Tap the > icon, and you're taken to the Dropped Pin's Info screen. In addition to the options offered in a regular Info screen, this screen includes a Remove Pin button for doing just that.

tip Why would you want to bookmark a movable pin? I often do this when I'm out and about and need to enter a couple of temporary locations. I may drop a pin, tap the blue icon, tap the Add to Bookmarks button, and then call the pin Where I Parked the Car. Then I'm at liberty to drop another pin during that same journey to mark a different important stop. Later, when I need to retrieve my car, I hope that I'm within range of a Wi-Fi network that broadcasts its location and can call up the appropriate bookmark.

■ **Show Traffic.** If the area you're viewing in Maps supports the Traffic feature (not all areas do), tap the Show Traffic button to see colored lines that indicate how congested the roads are. Green denotes good traffic flow, yellow is somewhat congested, and red is stop-and-go traffic (or sometimes just stop). Yellow and red areas on the map throb so that they're more noticeable. If the service isn't supported in the area you're looking at, the Info screen will read *Traffic Unavailable in This Area.*

tip   Be sure to zoom in on the map when you see yellow and red traffic warnings. The warning may apply to only one direction of traffic—with luck, the direction you're *not* traveling in. A zoomed-in view will tell you what you're up against.

Getting directions

Maps' Directions component is useful too. Feed it the locations where you'd like to start and where you'd like to end up, and it provides a reasonable route for getting there, like so:

1. Tap Directions at the bottom of the Maps screen.

   Empty Start and End fields appear at the top of the screen.

2. Tap the Start field.

   If you've used the iPod's Location feature to tell it where you are, the Start field automatically displays *Current Location* in blue letters. You're welcome to use that location as the start point. If you prefer to use a different start point, simply tap the field again and then tap the X icon at the right end of the field to clear it.

3. Using the iPod's keyboard, type the location where you want to begin your journey.

This location can be something as generic as a zip code or as specific as your home address. Alternatively, you can tap the Bookmarks icon and then tap a bookmark in the resulting screen; its location will appear in the Start field.

4. Tap the End field.

   Same idea—type a location or choose a bookmark (**Figure 8.7**).

Figure 8.7
*Entering start
and end points
for driving
directions.*

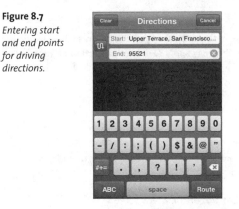

5. Tap the blue Route button in the bottom-right corner.

   Maps will present an overview map of your route. At the top of the screen are three transportation icons representing driving, public transportation, and walking routes. The Driving icon (the default) displays the length of the journey and how long it should take to drive—*279.9 miles 4 hours 57 minutes*, for example (**Figure 8.8**).

   The Public Transportation icon is likely to display different information from the Driving icon. It tells you when the next mode of transportation (which could be a bus, subway, train, or combination) is going to leave and when it's likely to arrive.

Figure 8.8
Trip overview.

 The Public Transportation route is intended for local travel. If you set Arcata, California, as your departure point and Parsons, Kansas, as the destination, the iPod will say *Transit directions could not be found between these locations.*

Tap the Walking button, and you see the most reasonable route you can make on foot (meaning no freeways), the distance, and the time it should take to get where you're going.

The Map, Satellite, and Hybrid buttons on the dog-ear page do exactly what you'd expect, but List's functionality changes when you're using the Directions feature.

Tap List, and the twists and turns of your route are laid out in numbered steps—for example, *1 Drive 0.4 miles then turn right at Old Codger Road. 2 Drive 2.6 miles then merge onto CA-94 W toward Tokyo.* Tap a step, and Maps displays that portion of your trip on a map, circling the important twist or turn outlined in the step as well as displaying the written driving directions for that step at the top of the screen.

To view the next turn in your trip, just tap the right-arrow icon at the top of the screen. To return to the map overview of your trip, tap the dog-ear icon; tap List; and then tap the Route Overview entry at the top of the Directions screen.

> **tip** When you return to List view, a purple circle surrounds the step in the list that corresponds to the portion of the trip you just viewed. If the fourth part of the trip was to turn left on Dankhippie Road, for example, a purple circle appears around the number 4.

If you like this turn-by-turn graphic overview of your route, you can skip the List icon altogether. Just tap the Start icon in the top-right corner of the route overview screen. The first step of your journey will be shown in all its graphic glory, along with the accompanying text at the top of the screen. Tap the right-arrow icon to proceed to the next step (**Figure 8.9**). Should you want to edit your route—change the start or end point— just tap the Edit button in the top-left corner of the display. The Start and End fields appear, along with the iPod's keyboard.

Figure 8.9
Taking a trip.

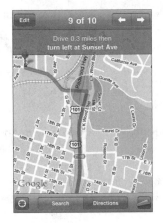

At this point, you can return to your journey by tapping the Cancel button in the top-right corner or plot a new journey by tapping Clear.

tip If you lose your Wi-Fi connection en route (which is likely), the iPod won't be able to track your location until you latch onto another Wi-Fi hotspot that provides location information. (Simply driving by one may be enough to update your location in Maps.) Fortunately, the direction information remains on the iPod; you can still follow the steps of your journey in List view, for example.

Location, Location, Location

I know—you've been staring at that small [icon] icon in the bottom-left corner of the Maps screen, wondering what on earth it's for. Allow me to reward your patience by telling you that this is the Location icon. Tap it, and the iPod attempts to pinpoint the iPod's whereabouts.

How Location works

The iPod touch can find itself via Wi-Fi networks. Some of these networks have registered their locations through Skyhook Wireless. When your iPod detects one of these locations, it can glean a pretty good idea of where it is. It will be even more accurate if it detects more than one registered network.

tip You can register your own wireless router with Skyhook. Just go to http://skyhookwireless.com/howitworks/submit_ap.php, and follow the directions to register your router's location. It takes about a month for registered routers to broadcast their locations to devices like the iPod.

Using Location

To pinpoint (as much as possible) your location in Maps, tap the Location icon. If the Location Services option is off in the General Settings screen, Maps will tell you to turn it on via a window that includes a Settings and

Cancel button. Tap Settings to go the Settings screen, where you can turn Location Services on.

The iPod will attempt to establish your location based on the information provided by the Wi-Fi networks around you to produce a map with a blue target that indicates where the iPod believes you are.

If the iPod finds you, first a broad blue area appears, followed by a smaller target with a throbbing blue dot haunting the middle of the target (**Figure 8.10**). Move around, and the dot moves with you.

Location's Long Reach

Maps isn't the only application that asks permission to use the iPod's location. Several third-party applications from the App Store use location in interesting ways—chat and Twitter clients, astronomy applications that calculate where the heavenly bodies are in relation to your position on Earth, and social-networking applications that broadcast where you are, for example. Before telling the world where your iPod is, these applications should ask your permission.

At times, however, you don't want to provide your location—such as when you've told your wife that you're at the office but in reality are poised to spring out from behind a couch and shout "Surprise!" at her 37th birthday party.

More serious security and safety ramifications may apply, of course: A youngster with an iPod touch may be staying late at school, for example. As with most things involving passing along personal information, grant permission wisely. If you're concerned about broadcasting your location, go to the General setting and switch Location Services off.

Figure 8.10
Location symbol.

You are here.

Weather

Weather is another iPod application that owes more than a tip of the hat to a Mac OS X widget. Though the layout of the iPod's Weather application is vertical rather than horizontal, it contains the same information as its namesake widget: a 6-day forecast (including the current day); current temperature in Fahrenheit or Celsius (selectable from the application's Information screen); each day's projected highs and lows; and icons that represent the current or projected weather conditions, such as sun, clouds, snow, or rain (**Figure 8.11** on the following page).

To move from one location screen to the next, simply swipe your finger horizontally across the screen. Alternatively, just tap to the right or left of the small white dots that appear at the bottom of the screen. (These dots indicate how many locations you have saved.)

Tap the *i* icon in the bottom-right corner of the Weather screen, and the screen flips around to display all the locations you've saved. To add a new one, tap the plus icon; use the iPod's keyboard to enter a location (again, a zip code is a handy shortcut); and tap Search. To remove a location, tap it; tap the red minus icon; and then tap Delete. To switch from Fahrenheit to Celsius, tap the appropriate icon at the bottom of the screen. To reorder locations, just drag them up or down in the list.

Figure 8.11
Weather application.

Voice Memos

Voice Memos is an application introduced with the iPod touch 3.0 software and compatible with the 2G iPod touch (sorry, 1G iPod touch owners). And yes, it's for recording audio. That audio can be recorded with a headset microphone plugged into the iPod's headphone port. To record and play back a memo, follow these steps:

1. Launch Voice Memos, and start talking—but don't record yet.

   Keep an eye on the VU meter at the bottom of the screen. If you see the needle move, the iPod can "hear" you. This needle isn't very accurate, though, so don't try to push it up near the red. If it gets anywhere near the –10 mark, you're loud enough.

2. Tap the red Record icon in the bottom-left corner of the screen, and start talking for real.

   A red bar appears at the top of the screen, indicating that the iPod is recording (**Figure 8.12**).

Figure 8.12
Voice Memos application at work.

3. Pause, if you like, by tapping Record again.

   To resume, tap Record one more time.

4. Stop recording.

   Tap the silver button on the right side of the VU meter, and your recording is saved.

5. Tap the List button in the bottom-right corner of the screen to play your memo.

   A Voice Memos screen appears, listing all the voice memos you've recorded. To play one, just tap it (and tap it again to pause). The timeline at the bottom of the screen displays the progress of the playback. You can tap and drag the playhead to move forward or backward in the memo.

6. Share it or delete it.

   The two buttons at the bottom of the screen—Share and Delete—are the means for doing those things. Tap Share, and a pane floats up with Email Voice Memo and Cancel buttons in it. Tap Email Voice Memo, and up pops an unaddressed email message containing the memo as an attachment.

7. Trim it.

   Tap the blue > button on the right side of a memo, and the memo's Info screen appears. Here, you can trim the memo by tapping the Trim Memo button. When you do, a pane appears that includes a yellow trim bar. To trim the memo, drag the sides of the trim bar to cut off the beginning and/or end of the memo. You can hear what's left by tapping the Play button next to the bar.

   To throw out the stuff you've trimmed, tap Trim Voice Memo. This action is permanent, so be careful.

   This Info window also contains a Share button, which saves you the trouble of backing up a screen to email the memo to someone.

8. Label it.

   Tap the name of your memo—*5:15 PM 00:17*, for example—and a Label screen comes into view. Tap a label that best categorizes your memo—Podcast, Lecture, or Idea, for example—and your memo is labeled. (You can also enter a custom label by tapping Custom at the bottom of the screen and typing a label name in the succeeding screen.) That label name replaces the time/date name in the Voice Memos screen.

When you sync your iPod to your computer, the voice memos you've recorded are transferred to your iTunes Library. Regrettably, the label names you've applied don't transfer as well. These memos retain their date and time titles.

Notes

Notes is the iPod's simple text editor—and by *simple*, I mean downright rudimentary. Tap Notes in the iPod's Home screen and then tap the plus icon in the top-right corner of the resulting Notes screen to create a new note. When you do, the iPod's familiar keyboard appears. Start typing your new novel (OK, novelette). If you make a mistake, use the usual text-editing tricks to repair your work.

Each individual Notes screen has four icons at the bottom. The left-arrow and right-arrow icons do exactly what you'd expect: move to the previous or next note. Tap the Mail icon, and a new, unaddressed email message opens in Mail, with the note's text appearing in the message body. Tap the Trash icon, and you'll be offered the option to Delete Note or Cancel.

To view a list of all your notes (**Figure 8.13**), tap the Notes icon in the top-left corner of the screen. Each note is titled with up to the first 30 characters of the note. (If you entered a return character after the first line, only the text in that first line appears as the note's title.) Next to each note is the date of its creation (or time, if it was created that day). Time and date information also appears at the top of each note.

Figure 8.13
Notes application.

Notes (6)	+
Addie's Xmas list	Dec 6 >
Apple Store shopping list	Oct 8 >
Birding list from Pt. Reyes	Sep 27 >
Book proposals from NP	Aug 30 >
Ben and Chris' plan for world do...	Aug 8 >
iPhone presentation notes for as...	Aug 8 >

With the iPod 3.0 software, now you can sync notes to your computer. If you've enabled the Sync Notes option in the Info tab in iTunes, your notes will be copied to your computer, appearing in Apple's Mail application on a Mac and in Microsoft Outlook on a Windows PC.

Clock

More than just a simple timepiece, the iPod's Clock application includes four components—World Clock, Alarm, Stopwatch, and Timer—that are available as icons arrayed across the bottom of the application's screen. Here's what they do.

World Clock

Just as its name implies, World Clock allows you to track time in multiple locations. Clocks are presented in both analog and digital form (**Figure 8.14**). On analog clocks, day is indicated by a white clock and night by a black one.

Figure 8.14
World Clock.

To add a new clock to the list, just tap the plus icon in the top-right corner of the screen. In the Search field of the resulting keyboard screen, enter the name of a reasonably significant city or a country. The iPod includes a database of such cities and offers suggestions as you type.

You can remove or reorder these clocks. Tap Edit and use the red minus icon to delete a clock. To reposition a clock, tap its right side and drag it up or down in the list.

Alarm

Your iPod touch can get you out of bed in the morning or remind you of important events. Just tap Alarm at the bottom of the screen and then tap the plus icon to add an alarm.

In the Add Alarm screen, you'll find a Repeat entry, which lets you order an alarm to repeat each week on a particular day; a Sound entry, where you assign one of the iPod's 25 alarm tones to your alarm; an On/Off Snooze entry, which tells the iPod to give you 10 more minutes of shuteye when you click the Home button; and a Label entry that lets you assign a message to an alarm (*Get Up, Meeting This Morning,* or *Take That Big Purple Pill,* for example).

To create a new alarm, just flick the hour, minute, and AM/PM wheels to set a time for the alarm. Tap Save to save the alarm. When you save at least one alarm and switch that alarm on, a small clock icon appears in the iPod's status bar.

tip   **You can create an alarm only for the current 24-hour period. If you'd like an alarm to go off at a time later than that, use the Calendar application to create a new event, and attach an alert to that event.**

Stopwatch

Similar to the click-wheel iPods' Stopwatch feature, the iPod's Stopwatch includes a timer that displays hours, seconds, and tenths of seconds. Tap Start, and the timer begins to run. Tap Stop, and the timer pauses. Tap Start again, and the timer takes up where it left off. Tap Reset, and the timer resets to 00:00.0.

While the timer runs, you can tap Lap, and a lap time will be recorded in the list below. Subsequent taps of Lap add more lap times to the list. When you tap Lap, the counter resets to 0.

Timer

The iPod's Clock application includes a timer that will tick down from as little as 1 minute to as much as 23 hours and 59 minutes. To work the timer, just use the hour and minute wheels to select the amount of time you'd like the timer to run; then tap Start (**Figure 8.15**). (Alternatively, you can tap a number on the wheel, and the wheel advances to the "go" position.) The timer displays a countdown in hours, minutes, and seconds, and the label on the Start button changes to Cancel. Tap Cancel to stop the countdown.

The iPod offers two actions when the timer ends: Either it plays one of its alarm tones (and displays a Timer Done dialog box), or it activates the iPod's Sleep iPod feature. The latter option isn't as odd as it first sounds. Many people like to listen to soothing music or ambient sounds as they drift off to sleep. The Sleep iPod option allows them to do just that without playing the iPod all night (and needlessly running down the battery).

Figure 8.15
*Time keeps on
tickin', tickin',
tickin' into the
future....*

Calculator

Unless you've stubbornly clung to your grandfather's abacus, you've
used an electronic calculator like this before. Similar to the dime-a-dozen
calculators you can find on your computer or at the local Bean Counters
"R" Us, the iPod's Calculator application performs addition, subtraction,
division, and multiplication operations up to nine places when you hold
the iPod in portrait orientation. When you choose an operation (addition or subtraction, for example), Calculator highlights the appropriate
symbol by circling it.

In addition to the 0–9 digits and the divide, multiply, add, subtract, and
equal keys, you find these keys:

- **mc** (for *memory clear*). This key clears out any number stored in the
  calculator's memory.

- **m+.** Tap m+ to add the displayed number to the number in memory.
  If no number is in memory, tapping m+ stores the displayed number
  in memory.

- **m–.** Tap m– to subtract the displayed number from the memorized number.

- **mr.** Tap mr, and the displayed number replaces the currently memorized number. A white ring appears around this key if a number is in memory.

- **C.** Tap C to clear the total.

Ah, but wait—there's more. Flip the iPod to landscape orientation, and you get a full-featured scientific calculator (**Figure 8.16**). When you rotate the iPod, any number stored in the calculator remains, so you can move quickly from simple to complex calculations and back again without losing your work.

Figure 8.16
The Calculator application's scientific calculator.

9

Tips and Troubleshooting

The iPod touch is a dream of intuitive design and ease of use. Yet nothing in this world (save you, dear reader, and me) is completely foolproof or infallible, which is why this chapter is necessary.

Within these pages, I offer ways to get things done more expeditiously, provide hints for operating the iPod touch in ways that may not seem obvious, and (of course) tell you what to do when your iPod does the Bad Thing and stops behaving as it should.

Getting Tipsy

I've sprinkled tips and hints throughout the book, but I saved a few good ones for this chapter. In the following sections, I show you how to control text, manage the battery, and sync your iPod efficiently.

The word on text

If one iPod touch feature frustrates the greatest number of people from the get-go, it's text entry. These tips will help make you a better iPod typist.

Keep going

Typing on the iPod's keyboard isn't like typing on your computer keyboard, a process in which you type, make a mistake, backspace to correct the mistake, and continue typing. Use that technique on the iPod, and you'll go nuts making the constant corrections.

Typing the first letter correctly is important, as mistyping that first letter is likely to send the iPod's predictive powers in the wrong direction. But after that, get as close as you can to the correct letters and continue typing even if you make a mistake. More often than not, the iPod's predictive typing will correct the mistake for you (**Figure 9.1**). To take the suggestion, tap the spacebar; the iPod will fill in the (ideally) correct word.

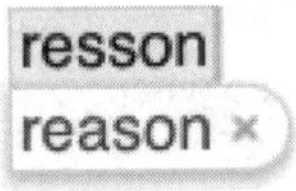

Figure 9.1

More often than not, the iPod knows what you meant to type.

Sure, you may need to go back and correct a word or two in a couple of sentences by pressing and holding the display to bring up the magnifying-glass icon, but doing this for two mistakes is far more efficient than retyping half a dozen words.

Move to the correct letter

You need to type as carefully as possible in one specific instance: when you're entering a password. As I mention elsewhere, for security reasons the iPod very briefly displays the last letter you typed in a password field before turning that letter into a black dot. This brevity makes it nigh-on impossible to correct your work, because you can't see where you've made a mistake.

For this reason, when you're entering passwords (or just typing carefully), tap a character and wait for the letter to pop up on the display. If you've hit the wrong character, keep your finger on the display and move it to the correct character. Only when you release your finger will the iPod accept the character.

Adjust the dictionary

Irked because the iPod invariably suggests *candle* when you intended to type *dandle* (**Figure 9.2**)? You have the power to modify the iPod's built-in dictionary. If you type *d-a-n-d-l-e*, but the iPod displays *candle*, simply tap the *candle* suggestion, and it disappears. Then finish typing.

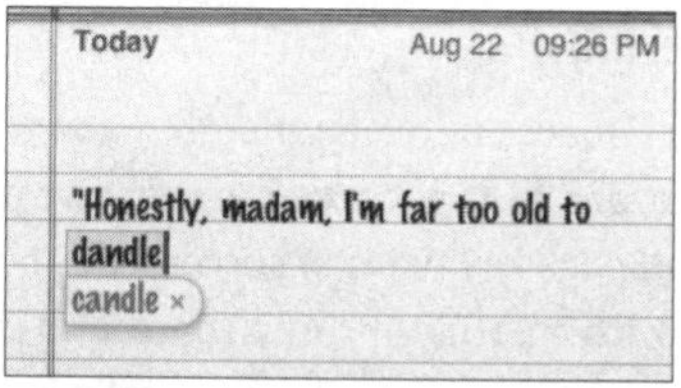

Figure 9.2
Correct the dictionary by tapping incorrect suggestions.

When you next get a good way into typing *dandle*, the iPod will propose it as the word to use. When it does, just tap the spacebar to autocomplete the word. The iPod's not stupid, so it won't suggest *dandle* when you next type *candle*, but it may not autocomplete *candle* that first time. In subsequent entries, however, it probably will.

Avoid unnecessary capitalizations and contractions

The iPod tries to make as much sense as possible from your typing. When it's willing to, let it carry the load. You probably won't type the letter *i* all by itself unless you mean *I*, for example. The iPod knows this and will make a lone *i* a capital *I*. Similarly, type *ill*, and even if you're trying to say that you're not feeling well, the iPod will suggest *I'll*. Conversely, if you're feeling fine, the iPod allows you to type *well* without suggesting *we'll*. Knowing that both *its* and *it's* are common, the iPod will never suggest the contraction.

Rule of thumb: When a word that can also be spelled as a contraction is tossed at the iPod, it will suggest the more commonly used word (**Figure 9.3**).

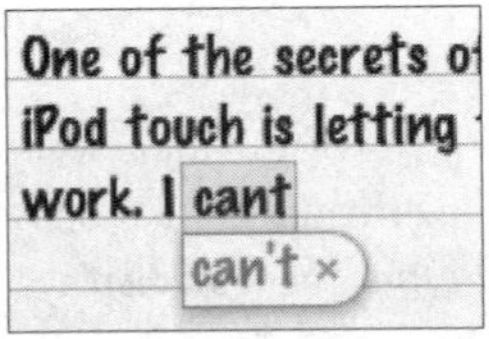

Figure 9.3
You can often skip the apostrophes when typing on the iPod.

One of the secrets o
iPod touch is letting
work. I cant
can't ×

Space out your periods

No, I don't mean place spaces between them. I mean when you reach the end of a sentence, don't bother going to the .?123 keyboard to enter a period. Just tap the Space key twice in succession. The iPod will end the last word you typed with a period, insert a space, and configure the Shift key so that the next letter you type will be capitalized. Now you're ready to type the next sentence.

tip You can turn off this double-tap Space-key behavior by switching the setting off in the Keyboard portion of the General setting.

Use Pogue's punctuation tip

The New York Times' technology columnist, David Pogue, revealed this tip scant days after the first version of the iPhone was released (it works on the iPod touch too), and in doing so, he proclaimed that other technology writers would use it in a heartbeat because it's so good.

Darn tootin', say I. It goes like this:

You may find it distracting to have to tap in and tap out of the iPod's number/punctuation screen whenever you want to add a stray comma or type *9* rather than *nine*. This dance isn't necessary. Just tap and hold the .?123 key in the bottom-left corner of the keyboard. While holding down your finger, drag to the punctuation symbol or number you want to type. When that item is selected, let go. The keyboard will return to the alphabetical keyboard.

Power management

Wonderful as it is to have an iPod that can play full-length movies, you do *not* want to board a cross-country flight, enjoy the latest Harry Potter flick on your iPod, jump off the plane with the expectation of sending an "I arrived safely" email message to hearth and home, and be greeted with a dead battery. Power can be paramount in such situations. To help ensure that your battery will still have something to offer, try these tips.

Treat it right

Your iPod's battery performs its best in these conditions:

- **It's warm.** Lithium-ion batteries perform best when they're run at around room temperature. If they get cold—below 24°F—they don't hold a charge as long.

- **But not too warm.** Running a cool iPod won't damage the battery, but storing it somewhere that's really hot—say, your car's glove compartment when it's 95°F outside—can. Also, the iPod gets warm when you charge it and extra-warm when you charge it in a case. Therefore, don't leave your iPod in a hot place, and remove it from a case before charging.

iPod Battery: How Long and How Much?

When the iPod was unveiled, many people worried because it doesn't have a removable battery. How long will the battery last before it gives up the ghost? And will you have to buy a new iPod when the battery dies?

To answer the first question, Apple claims that after 400 full charge cycles—that's a charge from dead to fully charged—the iPod's battery will function at approximately 80 percent of its original capacity.

As for the second question, just as you can with an iPhone (another device that's not designed for easy battery replacement), you can have your iPod's battery replaced. If the iPod is out of warranty—meaning that it's more than 1 year old and you haven't added an AppleCare Protection Plan, which extends the hardware repair coverage to 2 years—Apple will do the job for $79 plus $6.95 shipping.

By the time you read this book, you should see several third-party vendors jumping into the iPod touch battery-replacement business, just as they did for the click-wheel iPod. It's worth noting, however, that although some vendors may offer a "user-replaceable" battery, successfully replacing an iPod touch's battery on your own is more than a little challenging. The battery is soldered in place. Unless you're *very* good with a soldering iron or couldn't care less about destroying your iPod, have a professional do the job.

Lock it

The iPod isn't supposed to do anything unless you touch its display or press its Home button, but you might accidentally do one thing or the other if the iPod is rattling around loose in your pocket or pocketbook. Rather than project all 216 minutes of *Lawrence of Arabia* to the inside of your pants pocket, quickly press the Sleep/Wake button to lock your iPod.

Turn off Sound Check and EQ

The iPod features Sound Check and EQ (equalizer) require more processing power from your iPod, in turn pulling more power from your battery. If you've applied EQ settings in iTunes to the tracks that will play on your iPod, you must set the iPod's EQ setting to Flat, which essentially tells the iPod to ignore any EQ settings imposed by iTunes. To make EQ Flat, choose Settings > iPod > EQ, and tap Flat in the EQ screen.

Turn off Wi-Fi

Turning off Wi-Fi can help you get more life from your iPod charge. To turn off Wi-Fi, go to the Settings screen, tap Wi-Fi, and flip the toggle switch to Off.

Turn off Bluetooth

Yes, Bluetooth can stress a battery too. Turn it off by going to the General setting, tapping Bluetooth, and flicking the switch in the resulting Bluetooth screen to Off.

Turn off Location Services

This option is another one that can drain a battery as the iPod looks around every so often to see where it is. You can turn Location Services off in the General setting.

Fetch mail less often

Push mail and accounts configured to fetch messages automatically every 15 minutes will tax your battery's charge. If you don't need your mail Right Now, turn push mail off and configure mail fetching so that it's done manually (when you launch the Mail application). You do this in the Fetch New Data screen within the Mail, Contacts, Calendars setting.

Plug it in

If you're accustomed to the way that click-wheel iPods work, you may be under the impression that when you jack your iPod touch into your computer's USB port, you can't use it. Wrong. When it's plugged into its power supply, your computer, or an accessory device that supplies power, the iPod is completely usable. There's no need to unmount it to watch movies, surf the Net, or get email; everything works.

Sync different

Ask Apple about syncing your iPod touch, and the answer you get is simple: one iPod touch, one computer. But that answer's not entirely correct. To avoid that sinking feeling, keep these syncing tips in mind.

Sync to multiple computers

When you plug your iPod touch into your computer, select it in iTunes' Source list, and click the Summary tab, you'll see (under Options) that you can Manually Manage Music and Videos. On click-wheel iPods and the iPod shuffle, enabling this option means that on any computer to which the iPod is connected, you can add music to the iPod by dragging it from the iTunes Library to the iPod's icon in the Source list.

This isn't the case with the iPod touch. You can use this technique on only one computer: the computer that the iPod is synced with. Try it on a different computer, and you'll be told that the iPod can be synced with only one iTunes Library. To add music from the currently connected computer, you must erase all the media from the iPod.

Although the iPod touch lacks a click-wheel iPod's manual-syncing option, you *can* sync your iPod touch with different computers—to a point. The trick is that in nearly all cases, each computer will sync a different kind of media. You can sync music and videos from Computer A, photos from Computer B, podcasts from Computer C, and contacts and calendars from all three.

For this technique to work, you must enable the sync option in iTunes for just the media you intend to sync from a particular computer. So on Computer A, enable just the Sync Music, Sync TV Shows, and Sync Movies options. On Computer B, uncheck these options but check Sync Photos. Disable all these sync options on Computer C but enable the sync option for podcasts.

Sync from multiple computers to one iPod

You can add contact, calendar, mail-account, and bookmark data from all these computers to a single iPod. To do so, follow these steps:

1. Click the Info tab in iTunes' iPod Preferences window, and enable the sync options you want (Sync Address Book Contacts and Sync iCal Calendars, for example).

2. In the Advanced area at the bottom of this window, where you see *Replace Information on This iPod*, do *not* enable the options for contacts and calendars.

3. Click Apply.

   A dialog box will appear, asking whether you'd like to replace the information on your iPod with the information on the currently connected computer or to merge the data on this computer with the data that's currently on the iPod.

4. Click Merge.

The chosen information on the computer will be merged with the existing information on the iPod.

iPod gone missing

The iPod is small enough and out of your pocket enough that it's easy to misplace. Whether it slipped behind a couch cushion or you left it in the back of a cab, you'd like to know where it is. The Find My iPod feature lets you do just that.

To use Find My iPod, you must have a MobileMe account, which costs $100 a year. Also, before you can use this feature, you must switch it on (meaning that you have to do this *before* you lose your iPod). Just follow these steps:

1. Choose Settings > Mail, Contacts, Calendars, and tap your MobileMe account.

I tell you how to set up a MobileMe account in Chapter 2, in case you haven't done this yet.

2. Enable Find My iPod by flicking the On/Off switch to On.

3. Open your computer's Web browser, and travel to http://me.com, which is MobileMe's log-in page.

4. Log into MobileMe by entering your user name and password.

5. Click the Find My iPhone button (the second button from the right, bearing a radar icon), and verify your password.

 Yes, even though you're tracking your iPod touch, this feature first appeared on the iPhone, so it bears the name Find My iPhone.

6. On the next page, enter your MobileMe password again.

7. Locate your iPod.

   In the page that appears, you'll see a world map with the words *Trying to Locate* . . . on top of it. If your iPod is switched on and near a Wi-Fi network that broadcasts location information, and if the Find My iPod option is enabled on the iPod, you should soon see a map with a blue circle imposed on it. This circle indicates the iPod's location (**Figure 9.4**).

Figure 9.4
Find My iPod has found my iPod.

---

tip Again, if the iPod's not switched on and within range of a Wi-Fi network that provides location information, Find My iPod won't work; your iPod won't be located.

8. Communicate with the iPod.

   Click the Display a Message button, and a window appears where you can type as many as 160 characters. If you know that you've left your iPod in a place where someone may find it—a restaurant or a doctor's office, for example—type something polite in this field, such as *Please return my iPod by calling 555-555-1212. Thank you.*

To help get the finder's attention when communicating with a 2G iPod touch (this feature isn't available on a 1G iPod touch), enable the Play a Sound for 2 Minutes with This Message option in this window. The message appears on the iPod's display with an OK button below that dismisses the window (**Figure 9.5**).

Figure 9.5
Let the iPod's finder know that you're on his trail.

tip The Play a Sound for 2 Minutes with This Message option is perfect for those times when you know that your 2G iPod touch is in your house somewhere, but you can't find it.

9. Lock your iPod.

If you think there's some possibility that you'll get your iPod touch back, click the Remote Lock button and enter a four-digit passcode. This prevents the person who has the iPod from accessing its data. Later, when it's back in your possession, you can unlock it with this passcode.

10. If all else fails, wipe the iPod.

    If you're certain that the iPod is lost or in the wrong hands, you should wipe its data. To do that, click the Remote Wipe button in the Find My iPhone screen (refer to Figure 9.4). This feature permanently deletes all the media and data on the iPod.

tip If you wipe the iPod remotely and later recover it, you can always restore its data and media by plugging it into your computer. Remember, iTunes keeps a backup when you sync.

Troubleshooting

The iPod touch may be an engineering marvel, but even engineering marvels get moody from time to time, and when your iPod misbehaves, you're bound to be in a hurry to put things right. Allow me to lend a hand by suggesting the following troubleshooting techniques.

The basics

If your iPod acts up in a general way—won't turn on, won't appear in iTunes, or quits and locks up—try these techniques.

No iPod startup

Is your iPod just sitting there, with its cold black screen mocking you? Try charging it with an optional charger (perhaps you have one for an older iPod) rather than a USB 2.0 port. If you get no response after about 10 minutes, try another electrical outlet. Still nothing? Try a different iPod cable.

Still no go, even though you've had that iPod for a long time and use it constantly? The battery may be dead (but this shouldn't happen in your first year of ownership, regardless of how much you use the iPod).

No iPod in iTunes

If your iPod doesn't appear in iTunes when you connect it to your computer, try these steps:

1. Make sure that your iPod is charged.

   If the battery is completely dead, it may need about 10 minutes of charging before it can be roused enough to make an iTunes appearance.

2. Be sure that the iPod is plugged into a USB 2.0 port.

   Your computer won't recognize the iPod when it's attached to a USB 1.0 port or a FireWire port.

3. Plug your iPod into a different USB 2.0 port.

4. Unplug the iPod, turn it off and then on, and plug it back in.

5. Throw the iPod into DFU mode (described in the sidebar "The Four Rs").

6. Use a different iPod cable, if you have one.

7. Restart your computer, and try again.

8. Reinstall iTunes.

The Four Rs

In the following pages, I repeatedly refer to four troubleshooting techniques: resign, restart, reset, and restore. In order of seriousness (and desirability), they are

- **Resign.** Force-quit the current application by holding down the Home button for about 6 seconds. This step should get you out of a frozen application and return you to the iPod's Home screen.

(continued on next page)

The Four Rs (continued)

- **Restart.** Turn the iPod off and then on. Hold down the Sleep/Wake button until a red slider appears that reads *Slide to Power Off*. Slide the slider, and the iPod shuts off. Now press the Sleep/Wake button to turn on the iPod.

- **Reset.** Press and hold the Home and Sleep/Wake buttons for about 10 seconds—until the Apple logo appears—and then let go. This step is akin to resetting your computer by holding down its power switch until it's forced to reboot.

- **Restore.** Plug your iPod into your computer, launch iTunes, select the iPod in iTunes' Source list, click the Summary tab, and click the Restore button. This step wipes out all the data on your iPod and installs a clean version of its operating system.

If iTunes can't see the iPod, you need to throw the iPod into DFU (Device Firmware Upgrade) mode. To do that, plug the iPod into your computer with the USB cable, and press and hold Sleep/Wake and Home until you see the Apple logo. Then let go of the Sleep/Wake button and continue holding the Home button for 10 seconds. iTunes should tell you that the iPod is in recovery mode, and you should be able to restore it.

Fortunately, iTunes makes a backup of your information data (contacts, calendar events, notes, applications, and so on) when it syncs the iPod. After restoring the iPod, you'll be asked whether you want to restore it from this previously saved data. In most cases, you do. If, after restoring from your backup, the iPod continues to misbehave, restore again—but this time when you're offered the chance to restore from a backup, choose to set the iPod up as a new iPod.

Unresponsive (and uncooperative) applications

Just like the programs running on your computer, your iPod's applications—both those from Apple and third-party applications that you obtain from the App Store—can act up, freezing or quitting unexpectedly. You can try a few things to nudge your iPod into action. If the first step doesn't work, march to the next.

1. Resign from the application.

   If an application refuses to do anything, it's likely frozen. The only way to thaw it is to force it to quit. Press and hold the Home button until you return to the Home screen.

2. Restart your iPod.

   Some applications misbehave until you shut down the iPod and then restart it.

3. Clear Safari's cache.

   If you find that Safari quits suddenly, something in its cache may be corrupted, and clearing the cache may solve the problem. To do so, tap Settings in the Home screen; then tap Safari; and in the Safari Settings screen, tap Clear Cache.

4. Reset the iPod by holding down the Home and Sleep/Wake buttons until you see the Apple logo.

5. Delete and reinstall troublesome third-party applications.

   If a third-party application quits time and again, tap and hold it until it and the other icons start wiggling. Tap the X in the application icon's top-left corner to remove it from the iPod. Go to the App Store, locate the application, and download it again. Apple keeps a record of your application purchases, so don't worry; you won't have to pay for it again.

6. On the iPod, go to the General setting; tap Reset; and then tap Reset All Settings.

   This step resets the iPod's preferences but doesn't delete any of your data or media.

7. In that same Reset screen, tap Erase All Content and Settings (**Figure 9.6**).

Figure 9.6
Erasing all the content and settings from your iPod is the next-to-last resort.

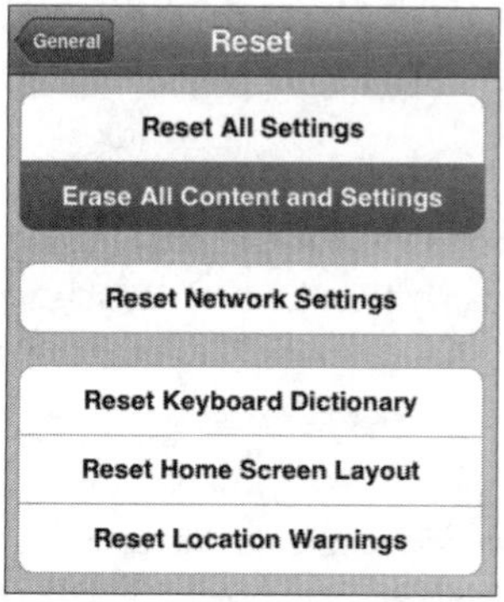

General   Reset

Reset All Settings

Erase All Content and Settings

Reset Network Settings

Reset Keyboard Dictionary

Reset Home Screen Layout

Reset Location Warnings

note   This step vaporizes not only the iPod's preferences, but its media content as well. Before doing this, try to sync your iPod so that you can save any events, contacts, bookmarks, and photos you've created, as well as the third-party applications.

tip   You want to try to back up third-party applications in particular because all the data for those applications is stored within the applications themselves. If you're unable to back up these applications and then lose them because you erased them, any data files you created with them are lost as well.

8. Restore the iPod.

   As I suggest in the sidebar "The Four Rs," try restoring from your most recent backup first. If the problem persists, something in the backup may be corrupted.

9. Restore yet again, but choose *not* to restore from a backup; instead, start as though you're configuring a new iPod.

   iTunes will install everything afresh, which means that you'll have to resync your data.

Mail issues

Are your attachments not opening? Is the iPod refusing to send your mail? Are you getting far too many offers for questionable nostrums and shady real estate deals? Read on for solutions.

Can't read attachments

You can read certain kinds of documents that arrive as attachments in email messages—specifically, Microsoft Word, Microsoft Excel, PDF, JPEG, and text files. But Word, Excel, PowerPoint, iWork, and PDF files won't open unless they carry the proper extensions: .doc or .docx; .xls or .xlxs; .ppt or .pptx; .key, .numbers, and .pages; and .pdf, respectively. Also, if the message body is formatted in rich text format (RTF) and includes an attachment, you won't be able to read the attachment. Try forwarding the message to yourself. This method should convert the rich text to plain text and allow you to view the attachment.

Can't send mail

If you can't send mail because your ISP prohibits you from *relaying* (sending mail through another ISP), as it may when you're connected to a Wi-Fi network other than your own, add a free Gmail (http://mail.google.com),

Yahoo (http://mail.yahoo.com), or AOL (http://mail.aol.com) account, and send mail via its server. These services are rarely blocked.

Can't cope with spam overload

The iPod's Mail program offers no spam filtering. If your computer's email client removes the bulk of the spam you receive, you'll be shocked when you download your first batch of mail on the iPod, because it's likely to be choked with spam.

If your ISP can't impose some kind of filtering on your email so that the spam doesn't reach you in the first place, sign up for a free Gmail account, and switch to it for email that you intend to receive on your iPod. Gmail has great spam filtering, so you'll get just the mail you want without the excess junk. (You can also configure Gmail to forward mail from other accounts through your Gmail account and remove the spam in the process.)

Index

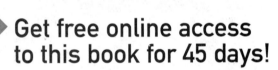